Preface

This book is about problem solving in school science and technology. While the National Curriculum is not to be ignored or avoided, there is no point in the book where we undertake a full analysis of either subject. Instead, in the chapters that follow, we contemplate the use of scientific and technological problem solving in a variety of different contexts within and without of the 5–16 age bracket for compulsory schooling. In doing so, the authors here offer up a shape and substance to the ways that many (most) of the requirements of the National Curriculum can be met without relinquishing all of the fun, freedom and fascination that comes from working with children on real problems in real classrooms. The book aims to detail some of this good practice as we explore the teaching of problem-solving techniques in a broad range of educational situations. It is not a book on 'how to do problem solving', more a collection of cases on 'how it has been done well by others'.

Within this there are three broad sections. The first is a general section where we discuss the nature of problem solving and provide a general backdrop against which such activities can be viewed in comparison with other teaching strategies. There then follow seven chapters by invited authors which focus on the teaching of problem solving in distinctive ways. Those in Section 2 take up problem solving in different curricular contexts – with an emphasis on problem solving for different types of learning. There are problems in intermediate technology, industry and the environment. Those in Section 3 deal with problem solving within different stages and phases of schooling – with an emphasis on problem solving for different types of learners: young women; high achievers; children with special educational needs and initial teacher trainees. The book is clearly aimed at practising teachers, teacher educators and advisors across all age phases, with specific appeal to those with a brief for science and technology education.

Mike Watts
Roehampton, July 1994

Acknowledgements

I would like to acknowledge the work of the 'Problem Solving Working Group' of the Second Latin American School for Research in the Teaching of Physics (ELAPEF 2, 1993) for their contributions to the thinking in Chapter 1. They are: Maite Andres, Marcela Aguirre, Jorge Antillon-Matta, Julio Blanco, Sonia Concari, Hector Covarrubias Martinez, Daisy Martins de Almeida, Marco Martinez Negrete, Marta Massa, Teresa Monmany de lomascolo, Antonio Saldano and Sayonara Salvador Cabral.

I am grateful, too, to colleagues at Roehampton Institute for generative thinking, counsel and advice: Grant Alderson, Arnaldo Vaz and Zelia Jofili. The photographs in Chapter 3 are used with kind permission of Intermediate Technology, except photo 1 which is used with thanks to Intermediate Technology/Neil Cooper, ITDG. The photo of Bill Cowperthwaite (Figure 3.4), is used with kind permission of the *Guardian*.

Problem Solving in Science and Technology:
Extending Good Classroom Practice

Edited by

Mike Watts

David Fulton Publishers
London

David Fulton Publishers Ltd
2 Barbon Close, London WC1N 3JX

First published in Great Britain by
David Fulton Publishers 1994

Note: The right of Mike Watts to be identified as the editor of this work has been asserted by him
in accordance with the Copyright, Designs and Patents Act 1988.

Copyright © David Fulton Publishers Limited

British Library Cataloguing in Publication Data

A catalogue record for this book is available from the British Library

ISBN 1-85346-270-5

Typeset by Franklin Graphics, Southport
Printed in Great Britain by BPC Wheatons Ltd, Exeter

Contents

This book is dedicated with love to Ruth

Contributors

Steve Alsop is senior lecturer in science education at Roehampton Institute. He coordinates the PGCE science course and the BA(QTS) science subject studies modules. Previously he has taught science in inner city secondary and primary schools. His research interests include the role of subject knowledge in initial teacher training and the public understanding of science.

Di Bentley is Assistant Dean in the Faculty of Education at Roehampton and has written extensively in science and health education. She is currently leading a research project in girls' understandings of energy.

Samantha Bentley is a recent graduate of Brunel University in Communications Studies and excels in PR work. For some time she was Information Officer for the CREST Award Scheme, and is now Examinations Administrator at Roehampton Institute.

Catherine Budgett-Meakin, is now the Education Programme Manager for Intermediate Technology. After two years in the Marketing Division of Unilever, and a year in Africa, she taught for 15 years in three Inner London comprehensives. With IT she has been developing a team to work on bringing the IT/appropriate technology approach into the Technology curriculum, using IT's project work from Africa, Asia and South America and providing unique resources on technologies from 'different cultures', and INSET support for teachers.

Tony Hamaker leads the TVE Team in Greenwich and is heavily concerned with both special needs through science and technology, and in developing industrial liaison through problem solving activities. He has been an active enthusiast on the science scene for many years.

Bill Harrison heads the Centre for Science Education, and the Science Exploratorium at Sheffield Hallam University. He has directed a major sponsored project on industrial problem solving for schools for many years and has a range of publications to his name.

Siobhan Walsh completed her MA at Roehampton (with an excellent dissertation) and is a teacher in Technology with the London Borough of Croydon.

Mike Watts is Reader in Education at Roehampton Institute with research interests in children's conceptual development, open-ended problem solving and teachers' professional development. He is a Fellow of the College of Preceptors and hopelessly devoted to guitar music, and the Welsh rugby team.

Alan West is the Director of the CREST Project and has written widely on problem solving in the UK and, with colleagues, he has recently produced a series of papers on the work of the project.

SECTION ONE

Extending definitions

This section explores the nature of problem solving, its constituent skills and capabilities

CHAPTER ONE

Describing problem solving: a core skill in the curriculum

Mike Watts, Roehampton Institute

Problem solving and learning

The opening chapter of a book on problem solving is the right point to start with questions and ask 'What is problem solving?', 'Why **do** problem solving?' 'What does doing it entail?' 'What is so good about it?'

The literature on problem solving is immense and covers such diverse areas as solving difficult managerial situations, psychological disorders, scientific problems, sorting money problems and much more besides. In this book we want to deal with schools, skills, tasks, teachers, concepts and classrooms, and so our answers to these questions will largely be in terms of the organisation of learning, knowledge and understanding.

Broadly speaking, problem solving involves 'actionable knowledge' – that interaction between thinking and doing which embodies the intermeshing of thought and action. The practical use of knowledge gives problem solving a relevance that cannot be achieved simply through abstracted conceptualisation or concrete tinkering. It encourages the transfer of knowledge across differing subject domains and contexts, and discourages learners from compartmentalising their knowledge. Problem solving motivates, provides enjoyment, stimulates interest and creativity. It puts decision making into the hands of the problem solver and this moves her or him towards increased self-confidence and personal satisfaction.

At least, this is the rhetoric. In practice, problem solving matches up to much of this for most of the time, as the authors testify in the chapters to come. There is now a growing body of research to show

3

that it really does motivate and stimulate learning (for example, Bentley, 1993). But it has limitations, too, since problem solving cannot be a panacea for learning in all modes: it has advantages but disadvantages as well. In this book, many of the benefits to schools and classrooms are discussed at length and whereas we may well all be guilty of dwelling on the positive virtues rather than the pitfalls these, too, are often evident in the prose.

Problem solving across the curriculum

There has been a rapid growth in the development of problem solving in schools. In part this has been due to its inclusion within a core of cross-curricular skills within the National Curriculum – generic skills that are appropriate regardless of content and context. It is true that problem solving happens in every field of human enquiry and form of knowledge. There are artistic, theatrical, philosophical, linguistic, journalistic, historical, legal and medical problems to be solved just as much as there are ones in mathematics, science and technology. It is an open question as to whether or not the processes, skills and procedures of problem solving are essentially the same in these different domains of understanding.

In the early part of the century John Dewey (1919) suggested five stages:

1. The perceived need for a solution.
2. The delineation of the problem.
3. The formulation of an hypothesis.
4. The rational scrutiny of the hypothesis.
5. Some empirical corroboration of the hypothesis in action.

At this level of abstraction, the processes of problem solving do seem to have some purchase in most areas of human activity. However, I believe that these just provide a very general template and that there are considerable variations within each domain: there is much evidence from research in science education to indicate that context is critical as far as problem-solving abilities are concerned. The best that can be said is that problem-solving skills in different areas are congruent: problem solving in history is congruent but not identical with that in science or technology.

Context dependence and independence

In the past decade or so there has been a growing understanding that thought processes may differ according to particular contexts and specific tasks. For example, our thought processes may be very different when describing a phenomenon in science to when reading Shakespeare, studying a graph or speaking in Spanish. And more than that, even within science and technology, our thought processes may be very different in trying to solve a problem about, say, making a model water wheel work in a particular way, from studying the life habits of Siamese fighting fish. Cognitive development is now considered to involve skills and knowledge that are pertinent to particular 'domains' rather than being a general 'capacity' or set of intellectual skills (Gilbert and Watts, 1983; Driver et al., 1985; Rogoff, 1990; Layton, 1991). In the language of cognition, learning becomes 'situated', it is relevant to certain situations but not to others. It is not that we necessarily want this to be the case; we often want 'transfer' of learning from one context to another but we know this is also quite difficult. This is not to deny that some intellectual skills are general and can cross over through many situations and contexts. It is, though, a rejection of the suggestion that **all** worthwhile cognition develops at a general level and is a re-affirmation of the importance of context in learning.

The transfer of skills is important. For example, if a youngster can use a particular set of skills in one situation, one would want that (s)he can then transfer these to another. This is not always straightforward and the understanding of ideas (and the motivation to disentangle them) can be constrained by the situation itself. In school, for example, there are many science and maths teachers who become frustrated that mathematical skills (say, drawing a graph) learned in the maths class are seldom transferred to the science class (see, for example, Zachary 1991).

In my view, knowledge has to be useful, and seen to be useful. Knowledge that fails to impress itself on everyday life in some way or other is untethered and irrelevant – easily surrendered and lost. It need not be wholly pragmatic and utilitarian since knowledge can be romantic, poetic and spiritual too. But if all one has is poetry, romance and spiritualism without the knowledge to avoid ill-health, traffic accidents, debt and disaster then life is all the poorer, not richer. In Layton's (1991) terms, it has to be 'actionable', and this is where problem solving comes in.

Hence, research in cognitive development has become much more grounded in the specifics of cognitive performance and, rather than suggesting that the skills and problems of thinking are generic, their specific nature and use in a particular context is being studied.

Problem space and conversations

Problems and solutions need to be considered in the light of the goals of the activity and the general context that surrounds them: what, for instance, is the nature of the problem and why is it important to find solutions for it? The structure of the problems, the knowledge that provides the resources and the solutions for effective or sophisticated solutions are fixed by personal and social purposes and values. Learners become active in their efforts to learn from observing and working with peers and the more skilled members of the immediate surroundings. They are both independent and yet sociable beings who develop practical and cognitive skills to handle problems – they learn **how** to solve problems by listening, watching and asking as well as through their own creative efforts. In this way learners explore, solve problems and remember their science and technology, rather than simply 'acquiring' memories or skills.

In the interaction between the problem solver and the problem, there exists a 'conversation' moving between the 'shape' of the problem (the problem space) and the agenda of the problem solver. A conversation sounds as if it should be words spoken out loud, between two or more people. However, as Hari-Augustein and Thomas (1991) suggest, individuals can have conversations alone in their own heads – as well as their hands having a 'conversation' with the materials they are using. As far as the teacher is concerned, this conversation must result in 'coaching' so that there is an enhancement of skill in particular problem domains. Ideally, for the teacher, the problem would 'lead' the conversation. One way of considering these conversations might be to think about some of the more common kinds of problems we solve every day:

- preparing a new dish for friends coming to dinner;
- using the bathroom with people who do not share your personal habits (wash out the sink; wipe down the bath; put the cap back on the toothpaste);
- getting down to writing and meeting those deadlines against the normal pressures of everyday life;
- replacing the headlight bulbs (or is it the fuse?) in the car;

- having to take a new class tomorrow without a clue for what to do.

To some extent how an individual solves a problem will depend upon their confidence, their self-belief about their own capabilities and talents, how well they have solved similar problems before and, therefore, their repertoire of past successes. It will depend, too, on past failures ('I'm not that good at writing'; 'I'm hopeless with electrical things'; 'I'm all fingers and thumbs when it comes to . . . .'; 'I'm not particularly artistic/musical/mathematical . . . .'). The conversations we have with ourselves, then, mean that we 'work through' the problem, chew over fears and foibles, rehearse 'scenarios' in our head, struggle with what is involved, plan for the task and for wayward contingencies, imagine the very worst, dream about the very best and so on.

But exploring the 'conceptual space' means more than just talking to oneself and worrying about the outcomes. There are ways in which tackling problems can be structured and there are a range of algorithms and strategies for problem solving. Some of these are discussed in the chapters that follow and each will have advantages and disadvantages. Most include some sense of setting out purposes; choosing from a range of ideas; making plans; organising time, materials, self and other people; checking rules and rule-abiding actions; putting plans into action; making judgments of success and then revising the plans and so on.

The main point here, though, is that despite algorithms and general strategies, we cannot treat learning as content-independent – we are not robots or computers who learn simple (or complex) routines regardless of the task or the circumstances in which it is to be undertaken. My cooking a new dish will depend upon exactly who the guests are coming to dinner every bit as much as how much planning and time I have left for preparation; sharing utilities in a household will depend upon how much tolerance I can muster for those who use the bathroom before me every bit as much as much as installing a shower, buying a toothpaste dispenser or hiring home help; planning for a new class tomorrow will depend upon my beliefs in my flair, spontaneity and confidence every bit as much as upon my preparation, management and knowledge of the group.

School science and technology

In science and technology, problem solving has been a success in shaping open-ended project work. Problem-solving approaches score well in devolving responsibility for learning to the learner, and in motivating self-direction and autonomy; they sometimes fail, though, to magnetise teachers because they appear 'uncontrollable'. The loss of strict teacher control is not always seen to be balanced by the sometimes uncertain learning outcomes. In practice, schools and teachers have been encouraged by a clutch of national schemes and initiatives, all of which provide problem-solving contexts ranging from industrial applications, environmental studies, information technology and 'alternative technology'. Work in mainstream schooling has received some exposure through a number of publications (for example Fisher, 1989; Watts, 1991) and there is now need to explore some of this work which extends towards the frontiers of the educational system.

Coming to terms

In this chapter I head for a description of problem solving and 'problem posing' and stay away, for a moment, from rank practicalities. I take up some threads and develop these towards an overall picture of what problem solving might entail in general terms. The chapters in Sections 2 and 3 of this book return to practicalities in some detail.

Problem solving itself can be seen to be a cross-curricular approach which entails a range of distinctive techniques and processes. It includes several ways of working and several modes of learning:for example, asking questions, building images and models, testing notions, investigating situations, researching topics, drawing on imaginative and inventive ideas and so on. There is a sense in which it has been championed by school science and technology, and most of the major national (and international) projects in problem solving have tended to be within these two areas. This gives a very pragmatic edge to problem solving which is often at odds with the other use of the expression: problems are what one finds at the end of the chapter or at the back of the text ('Open your books and do problems 1–13 on page 45' – or some such teacher exhortation).

However, this division between problem solving as the realisation of practical solutions and the rehearsal of abstracted exercises need not be the only forms of problem solving. There is a mode of problem solving – the Gedanken experiment – which trades on fantasy solutions in impossible situations. Nevertheless, for the purposes of this chapter (and others in the book) the emphasis is very much on the proposal and presentation of practical outcomes in both science and technology.

The basics of problem solving

At a recent conference (ELAPEF 2, 1993), a very busy working group set about delineating the central features of the nature of problems and problem solving. In this section I trade on their good work though the presentation here is entirely my own version. First, I want here to set out some notions for what a problem might relate to; second, to suggest some ways we can catalogue problems, their constituents and contexts. In different circumstances a problem can be some or all of the following:

- a challenge, an unsolved situation which cannot be answered immediately;
- some shortfall in knowledge or understanding;
- a personal or subjective state of mind;
- some change in thinking or conceptual strategy;
- the change or modification of some of the elements of a known situation – changes from within or outside of that situation;
- the generalisation or simplification of a known situation.

This list is not meant to be exhaustive but is indicative of the variety of instances which can be seen to generate problems. Problems, then, exist in many different forms and there exists a wide range of examples within school science and technology to illustrate all of these variations and many are suggested here and in other chapters. They can arise from:

- personal and individual thoughts and ideas;
- social group interactions and analyses;
- curriculum, workshop and laboratory activities;
- everyday experience;
- environmental issues;
- routine exercises; other peoples' solutions;
- cross-disciplinary interactions;
- commercial and/or industrial contexts;

- leisure and sporting activities;
- imposing new time constraints on known tasks.

These might be seen as fairly general 'problem opportunities' and of course there are many more different, specific, contexts in which problems can be generated. Needless to say, not all problems in all situations can be solved – some have economic, social and political implications that need complex initiatives at different levels to reach outcomes. It might be interesting to consider what criteria good problems may have in common. These might be:

- having 'possible' solutions which challenge and motivate learners;
- the generating of curiosity;
- the explication of clear unambiguous goals;
- producing cognitive change and the conceptual development of ideas;
- enabling intellectual, physical and social skills;
- favouring the transfer of learning from one context to another;
- producing a sense of ownership and responsibility;
- being suitably supported and resourced;
- generating creativity and innovation.

Models of problem solving

There are many models of problem solving and the most usual is a kind of cyclic or spiral process which encompasses:

- delineating the problem. This means setting oɪ t the shape and form of the problem and the major hindrances or obstacles to an immediate solution;
- establishing the criteria for success for the solution and the general constraints for the solution;
- the generation of ideas, the brainstorming stage. Usually the purpose is to generate as wide a range of possible solutions as possible;
- the choice of a narrow set of possible solutions and an appraisal of their feasibility within known resources, materials, knowledge, time and so on;
- the use of thinking and development from sources, expertise and resources transferred from a range of contexts and previous problems;
- initial trials and tests of the front-running ideas and a reasoned development of the most appropriate in the circumstances;

- the building and testing of prototypes which might be then modified to forge a cleaner solution;
- the evaluation of the result and/or a re-appraisal of the criteria of success at the start.

Just how cyclic or spiral is this process remains an open question. There is much to be said for the notion that all of these stages are present in learners' thinking all of the time but at different levels of awareness. To continue, though, I need to provide some examples, and then to pull problem solving further apart to delineate quite what it entails.

Problem types

While there are many examples of different types of problems in the other chapters of the book, it helps here to flesh out some terms. Let me begin with a chart as follows in Figure 1.1, a diagram that features again later as part of a bigger picture in Figure 1.4. Again, the labels there are not meant to be hard-and-fast definitions but some general descriptors of the different types of problems to be found. One example is the delineation of open and closed problem types. Open problems are commonly characterised as:

- having one or several possible solutions;
- generating a variety of plausible and fruitful outcomes;
- involving a range of appropriate strategies and processes;
- crossing subject and disciplinary boundaries.

In contrast, a closed problem can be described as:

- leading to one single correct solution, or a number of good results;
- having, usually, a numerical or quantitative outcome;
- involving a prescribed route to arrive at the end-point;
- holding within a single subject discipline.

The point of this picture is to put some broad labels on the enterprise without being exclusive. Moving through the levels of generality, problems can be experimental and/or theoretical and have varying levels of difficulty; they can be open or closed and can lead to one or more solutions.

For instance, an open experimental problem might be: 'to design and build a solar collector and measure its efficiency'. This is a project that could be tackled by A-level students on their own: less advanced

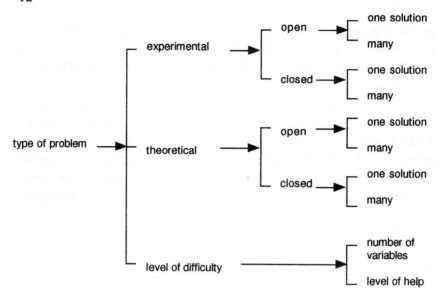

Figure 1.1

students would need different levels of assistance, particularly with the second, quantitative aspect. Similarly, to explore the biological effects of living near high-tension power lines (typically 60 Hz, 500 kV) requires a level of help and difficulty that would tax many young student. However, the measurement of the efficiency of rural systems, of the sort that Catherine Budgett-Meakin describes later in Chapter 3, are well within the range (in one form or another) of most secondary-school pupils.

So far, these are quite open problems and more closed types might be explanations of effects like thermal conduction and thermal expansion using both current scientific explanations and historical versions, or to make connections and reach some conclusions from tables of data like the the performance of several cars, hi-fi systems or the best ingredients for baby food, etc.

There are many banks of problems (see, for example, Watts 1991; CREST Award Scheme, 1993; Royal Society of Chemistry, 1990) and these are, of course, but a few.

Difficulties in solving problems

One might suggest that all problems ought, by their very nature, to be difficult. An easy problem is not really a problem at all – there is no real obstacle for the problem solver to overcome and so the problem is empty or vacuous. That said, the obstacles within a problem need not be all of the same type and any one problem may contain a wide range of obstacles to progress and/or solution. Using the kind of taxonomy above helps me focus on the sorts of hindrances solvers could encounter as they attempt a solution for a problem. For example, these might be:

● psychological hurdles such as:
  - the need for perserverence and concentration;
  - a positive mood and attitude towards completion and success;
  - motivation and a sense of competition;
  - co-operative and social skills;
  - coping with anxiety and insecurity.
● challenges to knowledge and understanding, such as:
  - the capacity to recognise and conceptualise the problem;
  - appropriate or unrelated frameworks of prior knowledge;
  - accurate or flawed perceptions of the context of the problem;
  - too little (or sometimes too much) information surrounding the problem;
  - the level of complexity or abstraction of the problem;
  - an appreciation of the models, analogies, metaphors and their respective limits within the problem;
  - the level of symbolic representation involved;
  - the level of creativity required.
● the need for skills such as:
  - methodological approaches to experimentation;
  - graphical skills;
  - numeric and calculative;
  - manipulative;
  - information processing;
  - linguistic/semantic.

I have not included in this list such difficulties as lack of time, money, need for outside expertise, or good working conditions – all of which may perplex a positive solution. These are, though, commonly particular to set circumstances and are not always general to all problems. However, this list is long enough – it is always possible for some of these to arise in combination and so make problems extremely complex. There are people who have no greater love than to tackle the impossible; and story-books and newsreels abound with reports and anecdotes of heroic adventures, which usually encompass solving enormous problems against all odds. It is always possible to create impossible puzzles, to apply increasingly more stringent requirements, more rule-bound constraints, barriers to success, and/ or complexities to keep the addict happy.

However, within education we commonly work within the realm of the possible since we generally want learners to succeed, and then to learn from success. Having looked at some of the difficulties, the question then moves to what kinds of resources or 'support scaffolding' can be put into place to help the problem solver – without usurping control or ownership of the problem. What can the teacher do to 'facilitate' learning through problem solving? Well, perhaps:

- helping to re-frame the question or problem area;
- providing analogies or conceptual models;
- delineating and de-mystifying some of the obstacles;
- re-constructing previously similar and successful solutions as suggestions;
- suggesting variables to control, giving clues in general;
- helping with experimental design, or discussing technical arguments;
- providing literature, resources or 'skill stations';
- asking pertinent questions, avoiding giving answers, answering questions with a question;
- helping provide access to expertise and expert help;
- providing general encouragement and support.

Structuring problems

Within all of this, we are commonly faced with how to choose or how to help learners choose appropriate problems. Which problem is best for a certain youngster? What kind of problem fits best with the curriculum, allows progression, develops particular skills and so on? There is considerable research to show two major features about problem solving. The first is that learners show more success with new problems where these are seen to be similar in structure to previous problems successfully solved. That is, if the student can see similarities to problems they have already successfully solved then they are able to see their way towards a solution of a new problem. The second feature is that, if learners don't see these similarities straight away, then they can also reach success if the similarities are pointed out to them in some way or other. This might be called the 'transparency' of the problem, that the structure of the new problem is sufficiently transparent that the learner can see through to the general formulation of the problem and so move forward towards some solution.

One way for the problem poser to facilitate transparency is keep within the same general problem pattern and then, for subsequent problems, to vary one of the central components of the problem in order to give it a new twist, then to vary a second component and so on, as shown in Figure 1.2 above for problems 1, 2, 3, 4, etc. This trades on the learner recognising the problem type and then appreciating how it is different so that this new problem can be tackled: 'Oh, this is like the problem the other day, except that it is . . . .'

In the same way, components can be removed altogether or new ones added as in problems 6 and 7. A further level of complexity can be the changing of the context so that the problem shifts as each context changes by degrees. In this case, the shifts require the problem solver to transfer knowledge and understanding from one context to another.

Contexts for problems

How can we describe the various contexts for problem solving? One common feature is the 'connectedness' of the problem to everyday life contexts. Unfortunately, not all problems within school life are of this sort and some – for example, those that come straight from the textbook – can seem contrived and quite false. There are problems set, for instance, which involve finding the time it takes to fill a container with water that has a hole in it and which leaks at a fixed rate, or to dig a hole which keeps filling up as the work takes place. These kinds of problems may have their place but do have a slightly farcical edge to them. Similarly, problems can be set that are based in mathematical terms and algebraic forms, and which can appear abstract and purely symbolic. Conversely, they can be contextualised in real live situations with real applications.

In Figure 1.3 these two dimensions have been placed at right-angles to each other to represent the realms of possibility between the two. The first suggests there is a spectrum of problem types from symbolic, abstract problems to real concrete practical ones. Too often science and maths are seen to typify the abstract, logical pole while the 'making and doing' of technology occupies the other. This is not the case, and the division between science and technology is much more complex than stereotypically portrayed. Both everyday problems and

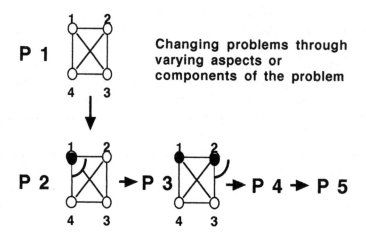

P 1 Changing problems through varying aspects or components of the problem

P 2 → **P 3** → **P 4** → **P 5**

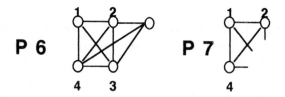

Changing problems through varying the relationships within and without of the problem:

P 6 **P 7**

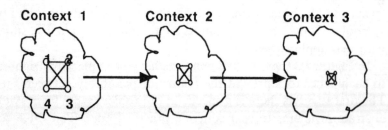

Changing problems through varying the context of the problem:

Context 1   Context 2   Context 3

Figure 1.2

Contexts for problems

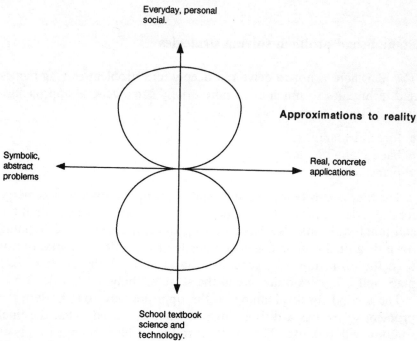

Everyday, personal
social.

Approximations to reality

Symbolic,
abstract
problems

Real, concrete
applications

School textbook
science and
technology.

Figure 1.3

contrived 'curricular' problems can be represented symbolically or set
within real applications, and there is a case to be made that any course
of study within science or technology ought to have a diet of each kind
of problem – not just one kind of problem exclusively.

The second dimension runs between two different contexts – from
the science and technology of school textbooks to the problems that
arise from everyday experience. There has been a major shift in recent
years to make science and technology more relevant to school
children's lives and, although this shift has been significant, there are
still many ways in which school texts and projects are wide of the
mark. The question here might be the balance that needs to be struck
between realism and curricular need, between concrete experiential
learning and symbolic abstraction. The loop imposed on the diagram
might be a trace that cycles through the four quadrants, allowing a
shift of balance with time so that teachers attempt to offer, and
learners attempt to solve, a range and combination of problem types.

A course design might follow some cycle through differing contexts so that the variety and applicability of solutions can be revealed throughout the problem solving activities.

Some broad problem-solving strategies

The plan here is not to delve too deeply into problem-solving tactics and techniques so much as to note briefly some general approaches. Broadly these can be described as:

- forward planning;
- back planning, and
- planstacking.

The first means being 'organic' and allowing the solution to emerge from a series of ploys. That is, not having a fixed idea about what the end-point will look like but amassing the components and building towards a final outcome as a composite of the different parts. In this way, the problem-solver generates the solution as the process takes place and evaluates quite late in the stage of things.

The second, back planning, is the opposite way round. Here the problem-solver has a distinct idea of what is needed, what the final solution will look like. The solutions to the problem emerge simply as details to be overcome on the way to the end-point: knowing what is wanted becomes a problem in achieving it past a series of hurdles.

The third variant, planstacking, is a combination of the two. Here, a series of intermediate targets are established with a distinct end-point in view. As progress begins, so work starts on several sub-targets. When progress is blunted for a while these are stacked and work starts on another – some sub-problems can be held as progress is made on others. This means having both a general picture of what is needed and allowing the sub-problems to grow and develop along the way.

There is no one way to solve problems and, although it seems that planstacking may be the more sophisticated of these three general approaches, it may not be the ideal way of working for problem solvers.

Evaluating and assessing problem solving

Assessment of any kind can be a vexed question and can lead to long esoteric diatribes from those both for and against various forms. Here,

I am interested in setting out some of the main educational points as they relate to problem solving without offering too much opinion about the necessity to assess, quantitative methodologies or the like. In the chart in Figure 1.4, the suggestion is that it is possible to trace any one of a number of strands to suggest possible forms of assessment. So, at one level, assessment will depend upon the type of problem, type of goals set, what is to be achieved, and the demonstration of the outcomes. These, in turn, depend upon greater specificity so that, for example, a 'theoretical' problem can have a single correct solution to be arrived at through several open routes; it might be reached through teamwork to promote new cognitive links and reliant upon formal representation. It might be presented as a report with the conclusions as numeric solutions. On the other hand, the problem may be an 'experimental' problem with a range of different routes and solutions, working under time constraints to develop an integration of ideas and expertise. This could be assessed by peer judgements through a group presentation of working models as a solution of their task. Neither of these two forms is either better or worse than the other, they are simply different ways of reaching information about the progress of the learner against a series of criteria for the task and the outcomes.

Many of these forms of assessment are part and parcel of the normal approaches undertaken in many schools and need no further elaboration. Other assessments of problem solving often take place in projects where there is a competitive edge and the 'winners' are they who meet the criteria best, fastest, highest, most aesthetically, economically, etc. These are criteria which tend to be very specific to the particular requirements of the competition.

Final comments

I began this chapter with a discussion of theory and practice, and one of the distinctions made in Figure 1.1 earlier, is of that between experimental or practical problems and abstract or theoretical ones. In science and technology we need both the theory and the practice – and these kinds of problems make different demands on the problem-solver. It is a distinction dogged with difficulties and dilemmas. There is a tendency in some quarters to value most those intellectual problems which are most abstract, closest to 'mental' problem solving and to de-value manipulative (manual) skill-based practical activity. It is this kind of division which Layton (1991) tackles so vigorously,

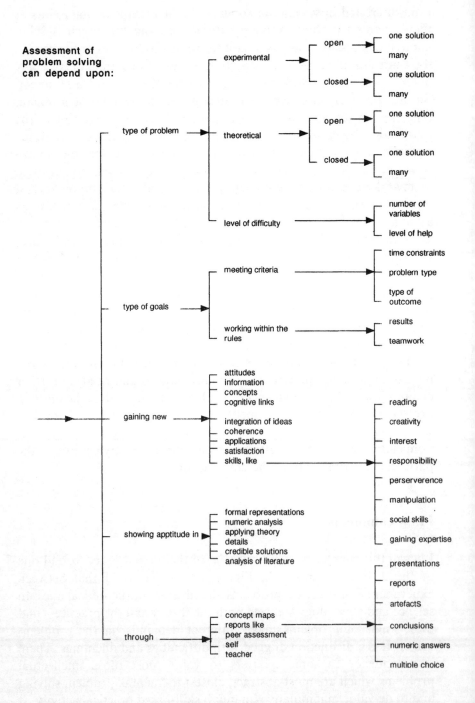

Figure 1.4

arguing that actionable knowledge bridges that divide to emphasise to conjunction of thought and action.

Just because a teacher presents a pupil with a so-called problem does not mean that it will automatically qualify as one for the recipient. There is a dividing line between a school-imposed task and a team- or personally-owned problem, and this line is not always easy to see. The teacher has an investment in asking the pupil to tackle a range of different kinds of problems from traditional calculative exercise problems to open-ended investigative problems, and must gauge the dividing line carefully. Ownership is important, as are the goals, the skills and processes achieved in the search for the solutions. In this chapter I have discussed some of the shape and purpose of problem solving.

To summarise some of the discussion in this chapter, I might voice one of the great fears teachers express about school problem solving: 'This is all very well, but exactly how much science (or technology) do they (pupils) actually learn?' There are several parts to this:

- handing over responsibility to others is risky and the outcomes cannot be guaranteed; pupils may well be responsible for their own learning but teachers are responsible to Headteachers, school governors, parents;
- lots of pupil activity can mask real 'on-task, academic learning'. Teachers feel many pupils are happy to hide behind a smoke-screen of seemingly purposeful process without 'really getting down' to things;
- teachers commonly find it easier to 'deliver' what should be learnt by taking control of matters and standing telling pupils the central features of importance, the facts, the main points, the right answers;
- open problem solving can have a variety of solutions which need to be judged in the light of their context and situation – teachers may feel exposed and vulnerable on unfamiliar ground and lacking in direct subject expertise.

As Hari-Augustein and Thomas (1991) argue, this is a tension between 'intentions' and 'learning'. Or, the intentions of the teacher against the intentions of the learner. These two may not always be at odds with each other but certainly often enough to make teaching a challenging career.

There is precious little research to furnish the powerful arguments to allay the fears and tensions mentioned above. Where case-study work is acceptable research, then this can add to our store of knowledge and understanding. Such is the nature of the chapters in the central sections of the book – they are cases of good work in differing scholastic contexts. All-in-all, it is our belief that open-ended task-based scientific and technological problem solving provides a powerful 'envelope of opportunity' for teachers and students to engage in productive processes and mature academic learning, putting knowledge into action for a purpose that suits the moment. The chapters that follow will flesh out the examples and contexts in which problem solving is realised in a variety of educational contexts.

CHAPTER TWO

A model for technological 'capability' in problem solving

Siobhan Walsh, London Borough of Croydon

Capability is a term that has particular meanings. A capable person (able, adroit, achieving, problem solving) is usually seen as someone who has some capability (skills, knowledge, judgements and personal skills) that allow him or her to succeed in certain contexts. In this chapter I want to explore the meaning of the term as it relates to Design and Technology in schools. While the subject area is called 'Design and Technology' I am going to to refer to more general skills of capability and draw them under the umbrella term 'technology'.

The background to the discussion in this chapter revolves around the shape of the National Curriculum for technology and the continuing furore which this has generated in the country. I am less interested in the details of the statutory provision, in the politics and warring factions pressing for change, as in a conceptualisation of the nature of capability itself. Nor am I interested in defining problem solving (see Chapter 1), but to emphasise instead the component skills when pupils solve 'food technology' problems in the classrom. I am keen to focus on that interaction between thought and action as youngsters tackle problems in the classroom or workshop.

The components of capability

Technology in schools is basically procedural in nature and so, in order to examine the relationship between 'process' and 'capability', a shift in emphasis is required away from analysing the end-products of problem solving – the outcomes of the process – to the thinking and decision making that form the product in the first place. In this way, the 'how' and 'why' of doing take on greater importance than the 'what'. I believe that the essence of a technological approach to problem solving can be seen in the interaction between the mind and eye which comes to be expressed through action.

This forms the basis of the SEAC (1992) model of capability. It is a model structured as an iterative process, moving from the **cognitive** to the **communicative** throughout the process. The core qualities that make up capability within the model are:

- *Cognitive understanding*, which includes kno ledge, understanding and cognitive modelling, that is the creation and shaping of ideas in the mind.
- *Communication* which is the expressing of ideas through a variety of mediums and should lead to greater clarity, depth and dimension.
- *Process* – This is the activity through which the pupil works and it is made up of different procedural qualities, identifying needs, developing proposals and appraising. The process enables the ideas to be brought into concrete reality.
- *Values and judgements* – These are the means of moving through the iterative process going from the reflective to the active.
- *Personal qualities* – Technology is seldom a solitary activity; these are the personal skills required to work effectively in a team.

The interdependence of these five qualities makes up an holistic concept of technology capability. The next step in understanding the model is to examine how the notion of 'progression' fits in. Progression is commonly seen as the step-by-step improvement in a learner's achievements as he or she moves through a body of work. Improvement, of course, might take place in any one of the core qualities and may or may not progress at the same rate in one quality compared with any other.To this end, technology capability might be imagined as a cylinder made up of five interlocking bands that represent the core above. If one quality is removed then the cylinder condenses. In this way, they cannot exist without each other, which gives sense to the expression 'holisitic Design and Technology' capability. Taking a cross- section of one of the bands it can be seen that inside there are many strands, rather like the wires in a flex. These strands are characteristics of that particular core quality. Progression is achieved when the child engages in an activity that calls upon the use of either a whole core quality or one or more of the strands within it. As the core qualities or strands are used they increase in breadth and length and in this way develop the overall dimensions of technology capability.

While true technological capability can only exist if **all** the qualities are represented, it is clear that not every classroom activity will develop all the core qualities at the same rate. Some activities will be specifically structured to develop a particular aspect, skill, or area of knowledge. In this way technological capability grows *en route*, through engaging in the activities rather than being an end product, and at any one time various parts of that capability may be more highly developed than others. A diagram of this is presented in Figure 2.1.

In a recent effort (Walsh, 1992) to test the validity of this model I defined the characteristics of two core attributes – cognitive capability and communication capability – and two characteristics from procedural capability – recognising issues in relation to human needs, and appraisal. In this chapter I put most emphasis on the first of these, though I spend a brief time looking at the other three. From this, I attempt to investigate whether these characteristics could be identified in the learning experiences of children in the classroom. I return throughout the discussion to the concept of iteration and what this means in practice.

The search for evidence

Principally, in my study, I was looking for evidence that shows capability in the operation of the design process with applied knowledge and understanding. It was not the initial premise of my work to make judgements about the resulting levels of capability but, rather, to attempt to view the problem-solving process through a series of windows. In so doing I wanted to identify the characteristics used in actually achieving capability. My research therefore sought to achieve two objectives:

● To provide evidence that the characteristics can be identified in pupils' technology work.
● To see how these characteristics are represented. That is, whether they can be identified as part of an iterative process and to try and determine whether they inform the pupils working through technological processes.

In order to arrive at this I undertook a comparative investigation based in two schools. In the first school I observed five children within

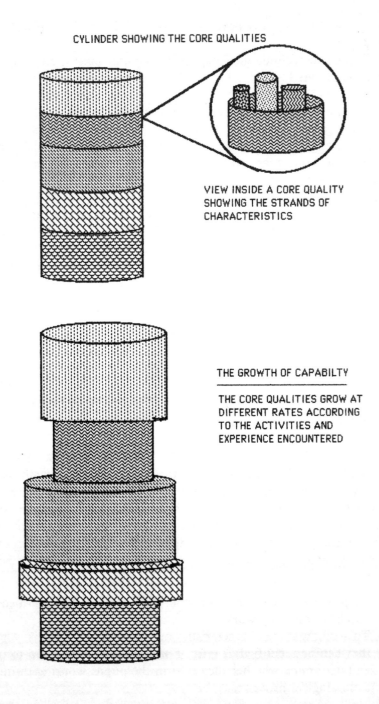

CYLINDER SHOWING THE CORE QUALITIES

VIEW INSIDE A CORE QUALITY
SHOWING THE STRANDS OF
CHARACTERISTICS

THE GROWTH OF CAPABILTY

THE CORE QUALITIES GROW AT
DIFFERENT RATES ACCORDING
TO THE ACTIVITIES AND
EXPERIENCE ENCOUNTERED

Figure 2.1 The progression of capability

a middle-band Year 7 (11 year-old) class. The pupils sat in groups but worked individually. Their problem was presented as an open-ended brief which required them to: 'design a healthy snack for sale in a school tuck-shop'.

In the second school, pupils were taught in mixed-ability classes as they worked in teams of four. A Year 7 group were working on a brief to attract people to their local area, and Year 8 were investigating how food, colour, shape, and texture are used in acts of celebration. This latter project was based on an exhibition 'The skeleton at the Feast' which explores the festival of the dead in Mexico. That is, throughout each of these different contexts, the problems posed to the pupils were clearly in the context of food technology.

Cognitive capability

The information presented here is a synopsis of my work, and I examine in turn evidence for the main characteristics relating to the selected core qualities. I begin with cognitve capability.

I defined cognitive capability above to include knowledge, understanding and cognitive modelling. That is, the creation and shaping of ideas in the mind. In studying these skills in pupils I have looked at strands within the core of the model, and these I identify as critical thinking, creative thinking, imaging and speculating.

Critical thinking

In watching the pupils working I decided, in the main, that pupils used critical thinking in three ways:

• in justifying their choice of work;
• in analysing the immediate situation to inform a course of action;
• in retrospective evaluation.

Let me take an example: two pupils were choosing items to cook and sell in an 'ideal' tuck-shop. In early conversations with the two, Puja and Lisa, I asked for the reasons for their choice of the dishes for the tuck-shop. They explained that the solutions they had chosen were to be low in sugar and fat, high in fibre, and therefore were suitably healthy foods. This showed a direct application of knowledge from research they had done. To choose appropriate dishes was one of the main (teacher designed) learning points of the brief. Later, in justifying their choice of cake, they offered further reasons (in these conversational extracts, R indicates myself as researcher):

Line 001   **R**. Why did you both choose banana cake?
          Lisa. Right, well, because banana cake, bananas are healthy and er. . .
          Puja. They give us energy and stuff
          L. That's right.
          R. Any other reason?
          L. I like them.
          P. Its easy to do.

In this case I see evidence of critical powers of thinking being employed in analysing the recipes in terms of nutritional content and then in making a decision. However, as later discussions reveal, there was some doubt in Puja's mind as to the validity of the justifications that she was offering. Although she appreciated that the dishes must have the correct low quantity of sugar in order to satisfy the brief and, while she knew that bananas are 'healthy' foods, she also recognised that she had indicated quite a substantial quantity of added sugar in her recipe. Because the teacher had given consent to her choice she seemed, though, to take this as confirmation that her recipe was nutritionally sound.

To set this in context, some earlier choices had been changed because they did not meet with teacher approval, albeit for reasons other than health (such as time constraints or skill level). This recipe was one that clearly appealed to Puja's personal preferences, a strong motivation for choice. Although there is some evidence that she used critical thinking in justifying the choice, its use seemed limited because, in the beginning, only a few criteria for judging the outcomes had been established. For Puja, these were, sugar content, ease of making and personal preference. She had then made the tentative hypothesis that the cake was suitable on these grounds.

When Puja came to evaluate the product (evaluation being a central aspect of critical thinking), her hypotheses was confirmed: the product did not actually taste sweet. This served to remove her fears about the quantity of added sugar since it was not discernible in the level of sweetness. So, although she felt the quantity added was too high, the fact that it could not actually be tasted made it acceptable. This exposes the limits to her critical thinking. What is important is that she recognised the disequilibrium between what she was suggesting and what she was interpreting from the evidence in the recipe. In my view she was too easily satisfied by the results, and preferred the teacher's restypictions to then going on to thoroughly investigate and probe her own concerns. The following extract reveals her acknowledgment of the discrepancy in her hypothesis. She now has the confidence to admit doubts about her choice, possibly because she feels she has already proved to herself the cake is healthy. From a problem-solving point of view, it would have been better for her to have arrived at the confidence to question and investigate at the time of choosing, which then may have led to a more critical investigation.

Line 008 **R**. When you were testing the cake at home what did you think about it?
Puja. Well I thought it was OK. In the beginning when I first saw it, when it came out the oven, I thought that it was going to taste not nice because it was all black and everything. But when I got home and it was all cold it tasted really nice.
R. What do you mean by nice? Can you describe it to me? What did you like about it?
P. Because it wasn't so sweet as I expected it to be, because I put lots of sugar in it and it wasn't that sweet.
R. Is that the main thing that you were aiming for? That you wanted it to be less sweet? Do you think that you achieved what you set out to do?
P. Yeah.
R. Just on the sweetness?
P. Yeah.
R. So if it had looked revolting but it wasn't sweet would that still have been alright to you?
P. Yeah (hesitantly).

The conversation then continues to show evidence of the use of critical thinking in evaluation. A second pupil, Lisa, interrupts to try and extend the criteria for judging the snack.

Line 023 **Lisa**. No I don't think so. Who ever saw it wouldn't want to eat it, you want to give a good impression when people see it.
Puja. Yeah I know impressions are the first thing, but sometimes people don't really care about impressions.
L. I know, but if you're going to buy from the tuck shop they wouldn't want to buy it.
R. So would you buy something from the tuck shop that looked revolting? (Asking Lisa)
L. Me? NO!
R. But you would? (Asking Puja)
P. Er . . .
L. See, see, you know it's right!

Another pupil, Cara, now joins the discussion adding a further dimension.

Line 034   **Cara**. If it's in some packaging how will they know?
Puja. [Unable to answer]
R. So you think that as long as the packaging looks all right then it's OK?
C. Yeah most of the time.
R. So you think packaging is an important factor in designing a good snack?
C. I don't know maybe you should try and work out a shape or something. If it looks disgusting, like my muesli bars looked a bit disgusting, then maybe if I had put them into a more interesting shape they might have been OK.

What I see in this extract is that Cara and Lisa are trying to extend the criteria for judging the success of the snack. Puja still has some difficulty taking this on board. Her inability to offer further criteria seems to be the result of a combination of factors. If she set up more criteria, there is then a chance her snack might not meet them all and therefore prove unsuitable – and she wants to succeed.

An important point in all the pupils' evaluation is that at the start of the work there seemed, in my view, to have been an inadequate exploration of the brief. The pupils had only a very limited notion of what comprised a 'good' snack and their solutions reflected the few issues described by the teacher. Full critical analysis by Puja of her snack was therefore severely restricted by the limited criteria established. To try and introduce more criteria once the snack had been made was being interpreted as criticism of her, and therefore difficult for her to acknowledge and use. The other two pupils did not have this same sense of criticism. Their impartiality allowed them to exercise greater critical powers. This defensiveness in tｌe face of discussion has real implications for classrooms. There must be an environment, suitable for the development of problem solving, where the best results can be gained in a non-threatening situation.

The second way pupils used critical thinking was to inform immediate decision-making, and this can be seen when Cara is tackling her practical work. She is in the process of making some Muesli biscuits when the mixture seems to be separating in the saucepan.

Line 042   **Cara**. Miss, this won't mix in, the sugar is still there . . . (teacher checks the mixture)
R. What is the matter with it?

> C. Oh, nothing at the moment, I just thought that there was something wrong with it. I just thought that the . . ., 'cos I thought that the sugar wouldn't sort of go in properly.
> R. How did you know the sugar wasn't going in properly?
> C. 'Cos you could still see the little fat bits around it. (Here she is describing the mixture where there is a lot of surplus fat in the pan not being absorbed by the other ingredients) . . . I have to try and get the margarine into this stuff (referring to the other ingredients in the pan).
> R. It doesn't seem to be going in. What could you do, do you think?

Cara decides to add some sultanas to the mixture and, when questioned about the effectiveness of this solution, she is able to confirm that the mixture has absorbed the fat. In this extract Cara is making judgements based on her observations. Through analysing the situation she has to decide whether and how to alter her course of action. Obviously there is some 'teacher' intervention, though she herself recognises the need for help and calls for attention. My questions also prompt an alternative to the problem, but it is she who decides what to add, and when enough had been done, to remedy the situation and enable her to return to the recipe instructions.

In these short sequences critical thinking has been shown in:

- predicting what should happen;
- analysing the alternatives;
- selecting a remedy;
- assessing the outcome.

In my report I identified various types of critical thinking as forming part of the model that makes up the concept of capability. I did not expect, in a short piece of research, to find evidence for **all** the modes of thinking but I was able to identify the following:

- *Hypothesising* – When they select their dishes to answer the brief.
- *Reflecting* – When they analyse what is happening.
- *Justifying* – When they give reasons for their actions or choices.
- *Evaluating* – When they review their work or, as was seen with Cara, when she had to decide on a course of action.
- *Questioning* – When they discussed with Puja the criteria for testing the snack.

Creative thinking

In seeking evidence of creative thinking I focused on such sub-divisions as fluency, flexibility, originality, and elaboration. In class I found some evidence of children elaborating ideas and showing flexibility. The former was seen when Puja was solving the problem of the design of the label for her snack:

Line 053   **R**. Tell me what are the things you started doing? You have immediately got a rectangle here on your page. Why did you do that?
Puja. Well it isn't really exactly a rectangle it is going to have round things, it is going to be like a square, a square container. We made up things on the board that we needed, we made up a list.
R. So your ideas came from the discussion, the brainstorming?
P. Yes.
R. At this moment in time have you got an idea of what the package will look like?
P. Yes.
R. How detailed is it?
P. Its got a few oranges on it, on the sides and its got ingredients and everything round it and how much it contains in it.
R. Right, so you've got the package, the size of the package in your mind, you've got oranges on the cover.
P. And the design.
R. The orange colour is the design?
P. And I've got the logo.

Towards the end of the lesson the teacher asks them to plan their homework. Puja is faced with completing her label design. She describes to me some of the factors she has to consider in order to complete the label.

Line 071   **Puja**. What I'm going to put like ingredients and how I should to put it.
R. What do you mean how you should put it?
P. Well if you look at normal packaging they normally say difficult words and stuff. They have things like vitamins and calories and all that and I have to find out how much its got in the juice I made.
R. Right so how are you going to do that?
P. Well I've got a little bit left so I'll have to find out, I don't know how I'm going to find out yet . . . from the recipe.
R. So the recipe will tell you the ingredients . . .
P. And how much calcium, and things like that.

R. Does it tell you that in the recipe book?
P. Yes . . . (stops to look up in the recipe book) . . . It tells you how much energy its got and um, fibre, fat protein calcium, iron and vitamin C.
R. So will you use all of that information or some of it?
P. I don't know, maybe some of it.
R. And how will you represent that information?
P. You know those, it has like a big rectangle, and it has two columns one what it is and the other how much and that's what I'm going to do.
R. Yes. You see here (referring to the recipe book) it is like a bar chart. Will you use a bar chart or . . . .
P. No.
R. Why not?
P. It's not what I want, because its hard to read when it's in a bar chart. It's easier if it's in writing . . . . you've got to work things out if it's a bar chart it's easier if it is writing, all you've just got to do is read it if it is writing.

When Puja began solving the task of designing the label she immediately began to draw the shape of the label on her book. There appeared to be no time at all when she reflected on the possible design. The immediate question here is: did she already have a clear image of the design in her head? The dialogue above would seem to indicate that she did have a basic picture in her 'mind's eye' which is conveyed in lines 060 onwards, though it is clear that through discussion more design details are added. When she starts to consider the homework (lines 071 onwards) the problem of how the nutritional information will be represented on the label begins to arise. There is no mention of this aspect of the design in the early part of the discussion. It is clearly an elaboration as the whole idea grows from the original simple design that included just shape, colour, size and logo, to one that offers far more complex information on nutrients and how this information will be represented. This presents her, too, with the problem of how to find out the correct information. The link between elaboration and fluency can be seen in the way her ideas suddenly emerge. When faced with a problem – such as how to find out the nutritional content – Puja appears to be stuck. Just as she is slowly admitting to this blockage, she hits upon a possible solution – as if during the time that has elapsed she has subconsciously been running possible ideas through her mind. The voicing of the solution elaborates the idea and allows her to go on and develop it further.

When looking for flexibility, as one type of creative thinking, evidence is perhaps seen in one of the earlier extracts, from lines 034 onwards, when Cara presents a new angle on possible ways to judge the successes of the snack. The discussion had focused on judging the snack by its nutritional content and taste, when she then brings in a new dimension, the packaging. She shows a degree of flexibility in the way she views the problem and in suggesting an alternative route. At first, she does not offer the idea as a solution just as an alternative to be considered. This is in sharp contrast to Puja who has great difficulty in extending her vision of alternatives.

During the study I had the opportunity of gathering evidence from a class in a second school. School 2 uses group work and here I found evidence for the fluency of ideas. The brainstorming at the beginning of the project enables detailed exploration of the brief. Pupils are encouraged to contribute possible suggestions about the meaning of the original question and how it might be carried out. The enthusiasm of the group is used to generate a flow of ideas (some more relevant than others) but at this stage all ideas are accepted to be analysed later. Here I still indicate myself as R and the pupils simply as A, B and C.

Line 096   **R**. So what do you think the question is about?
A. I think its about, um, how you see what Wandsworth is like. 'Cos I mean people don't think Wandsworth is all that good and then you can show others that it actually is.
R. And how would you do that?
B. By putting pictures up.
A. Advertising Wandsworth.
R. Right we said that we would work using food, how could we attract people using food ?
B. Those big posters of food.
A. Take lots of photographs of different kinds of foods.
R. What sort of foods? Would we just take photographs of any foods?
A. Particular foods from Wandsworth.
B. Make a cake and put a name of Wandsworth that my first idea and only idea . . .
A. Foods from Wandsworth.
B. Fruits and everything.
A. Foods that you would normally find in Wandsworth
A&B. Cakes chips, Kentucky, pizza.
C. Restaurants.
R. What sort?
A. Indian . . . .

My intervention in this extract clearly prompts the pupils, and from that prompting even more ideas flow. It is also possible to see the benefit of group work like this where pupils are stimulated by what the others say – and often elaborate the previous comments, rather like word association resulting in a steady stream of ideas.

It was difficult to find evidence of any really original ideas in any of the lessons I observed. By 'originality' I mean genuine novelty of ideas. However, it is important to take into account the structure of the brief provided for the pupils, since some briefs would be more likely to develop different ways of thinking than would others.

Perhaps the clearest observation to be made about these types of thinking is that, although I saw evidence of different modes of thinking associated with the model, these tended to be observable in isolated incidents and did not contribute somehow to the overall growth or progression of an idea. Perhaps this is understandable in School 2 where the teacher intended, and planned, a very structured (and therefore constraining) unit. But the teacher in School 1 was aiming at an open-ended project and here there seemed to be a lack of progression of ideas. It was almost as if the pupils went through the mechanics of the process but then they finally selected a solution from a set of preconceived ideas. So, although creative thinking can be identified at various times, it does not always seem to be applied in the final ideas chosen, with the result that the pupils' work seemed contrived in some cases. One example might be that of Puja, who chose three things to make for the tuck-shop, but in each case used the same reasons for choosing these. It is hard to discern any development in terms of the items selected.

The point here is that, in trying to track the growth of ideas – which is an important part of tracking creative thinking in school technology, it is sometimes hard to see the overall conception, the 'spin-offs', elaboration and flexibility within the whole project. They are there at individual times but they may not inform the overall growth of ideas in whole process. Some of this lies with the teacher and the choice of problems: although different practical activities were carried out, the underlying reasons and applications of knowledge were the same for each activity.

Imaging and speculating

I have tried to illustrate, with some moments of evidence, those parts of the creative thinking process which include the ability to image and speculate. One such instance might be the extract in lines 053 onwards, where Puja is designing the label for her product. As I pointed out there, she has the starting point of the design in her head and, through the discussion with me, she is seen to manipulate these ideas and elaborate them. The representation of this mental image is eventually conveyed through her model on paper, which is the drawing of the label.

Further evidence can be seen in the work at School 2 with Year 8 pupils, Sukima and Michelle, who are trying to create a dish for their brief on 'celebration'. This imaging is in both the creation of the dish (through the identification of the ingredients selected), and then the planning of the method of preparation. The images are presented in the form of a plan of action for the practical work and ultimately in the dish when it is made. The extract below illustrates this, where the pupils have just finished describing their choice of ingredients and now turn their attention to the method of preparation:

Line 117　**R**. Now what are you going to make the sauce out of?
Michelle. We could put tomatoes.
R. A tomato-based sauce, are you putting the tuna in the sauce?
M & Sukima. Yeah.
R. OK , so you are going to have pasta. And what else?
Su. Cheese and, er, herbs.
R. OK, tell me how you would make the sauce.
Su. Well we could . . . . you know take the tinned tomatoes and mix the tuna into the tomatoes.
R. Would you need to add anything for flavour like an onion?
Su. Yes.
R. Tell me how.
Su. Fry an onion, put the tomatoes and chop them up with the herbs and salt and black pepper . . . .
M. Tuna, add the tuna and let it bubble away in a saucepan, and the pasta in an other saucepan. Then mix it together and put cheese on the top.

The pupils are designing their own method, so each step shows the shaping of the ideas as a concept of the recipe develops in their mind's eye.

As I indicated earlier, many of the choices in the pupils' work seemed to be rather contrived. Not so much, that is, in the suitability of the dishes but in the reasons (and belief in the reasons) offered in support of their choices. For example, all the 'tuck-shop' foods were appropriate but was this by design or good fortune? Was it just coincidence that the pupils chose foods they liked, that then just happened to be suitable break- time snacks? Or had they made reasoned choices? Again, this may go back to a lack of exploration of the brief. Because many did not have a full understanding of the context in which they were working, they could not make realistic choices since the criteria on which they based the decisions were so limited. It could be said that, although the dishes satisfied certain criteria, the final range of dishes did not satisfy the full intention of the project because they did not represent all aspects of the brief.

While the model for technological processes suggests areas of knowledge, it also stresses the application of that knowledge in true achievement of capability. Within the classroom observations I made, I have already cited evidence where the pupils did apply knowledge from certain of the categories put forward in the model. These were understandings of such things as materials, where the pupils selected appropriate ingredients and manipulated foods using knowledge of their properties.

However, what is perhaps a little disconcerting is that, although there was some initial input of knowledge, it was not continued and developed throughout the unit of work. The result of this was that the pupils quickly fell back on their already pre-existing knowledge, repeating the same processes rather than extending them. Having pupils learn on a 'need to know basis' is good, so long as pupils are able to recognise what they need to know and when they need to know it. However, in the evidence presented here there is an argument for some structured input in order that the pupils can then apply this knowledge and develop further ideas. It is worth returning to the concept of capability, in that it involves the ability to operate the design process with knowledge and understanding – not just being able to execute the process alone. Merely operating the process with exactly the same knowledge base does not result in capability. It could be argued that the pupils in this study were repeating the process rather than extending their knowledge (which should in turn develop the process).

Communicative capability

At the beginning I described communicative capability as the expression of ideas through a variety of mediums which should lead to greater clarity, depth and dimension. In my study, the effect of the different styles of delivering Design and Technology was very evident in the types of communication seen in the two schools. In School 1 I saw the pupils operate as individuals, merely engaging in transactional conversation (except when I involved them in group discussion). In the second school all the work was undertaken very much as a team: discussion and sharing of ideas was positively encouraged. Obviously, in both cases, the ideas were eventually communicated through written work and the actual solution to the problems – the making of foods. The examination and detailing of the ideas was perhaps under-developed in the first school through pupils' lack of opportunity to communicate verbally about their designs. The consequence of this has already been illuminated in the case of Puja, who failed to give good justification for her choice, possibly because her ideas were never challenged until the final evaluation.

In the extract below two pupils, Sukima and Ben, are discussing how shape, colour, fabrics and food are used in celebration.

Line 133   **Ben**. Let's look at fabrics, clothes and decoration.
Sukima. Yeah clothes and fabrics like masks, wigs. They have certain types of fabrics in some countries for celebrations, saris.
B. They use some fabrics for decoration.
R. Yes, try to broaden you ideas to think of different types of materials.
B. Decorations.
Su. Wood. They use wood for coffins.
B. So you could have lines coming off decorations and list things sort of like flowers.

The passage shows the generation and development of ideas through the opportunity to communicate but what is more interesting is the point at which Ben begins to see the connection between the ideas, at which point he begins modelling them in a simple spider diagram. He started first just jotting down the individual ideas as they were called out but, later, he sees the connection between ideas and starts to group them on his page. The resulting diagram is then a means of communicating the evolution of his ideas with the others.

Earlier extracts such as Sukima (lines 117 onwards) shows how communication is used to tease out the problems of the recipe and ingredients and, before this, is seen when Puja designs her label (lines 071, etc.). The interplay of ideas in these two instances is a good example of the iterative process within the overall technological process. Here, reflectiion and action are working together in the development of the broad idea. Each time I (as the observer) pose a question, the pupil has to reflect using his or her internal cognitive abilities and then voice a possible solution through whichever medium is chosen. The idea is either rejected or developed, repeating the iterative process cycles over and over again until a conclusion is reached – resulting in the final idea being developed.

Process and judgements

In this final part of the chapter I want to round off parts of the model with a brief look at some of the processes and value judgements which lie within the the core of capability. Problem solving is essentially process-based and no activity is without value judgements of some sort. At the beginning I described these aspects as 'process': the activity through which the pupil works, and made up of procedural qualities such as identifying needs, developing proposals and appraising.

Let me dwell on 'identifying needs' for a moment, particularly where these relate to what is called 'human matters'. In order to satisfy a human need, usually there has to be an understanding of the context so the needs can be identified. As has already been pointed out, unless the context is explored very fully, then the identification of needs will be on a quite limited scale. Within the project on preparation of food for the tuck-shop there was, for instance, no consideration of portion control, cost, the maintenance of quality, market research, etc. However, the fact that even a **few** needs were successfully identified (such as nutritional need, taste and appearance) might be taken as sufficient indication of the importance of the characteristic within the capability model.

I have mentioned the ways that values and judgements pervade such qualities as critical thinking, and how this involves the process of moving through the iterative process, from the reflective to the active. In the schools I observed there is evidence of both on-going (formative) and end-of-task (summative) judgement and appraisal. For instance, Cara (lines 042 onwards) was seen to use formative appraisal when deciding on the ingredients to use in order to improve her practical work; Puja was engaged in teacher-directed summative appraisal in her work (for instance, her lines 008 onwards).

It is worth noting that, where there is evidence of summative appraisal, its value was not fully as the model intended. In the observations I made, the notion of 'appraisal' was used as a means of rounding off and concluding the project, whereas, ideally, it should enable the person to see further avenues of exploration. The final appraisal should be a new beginning, should inform and should not be an end in itself – as it was in the case of these pupils.

Summary of ideas

Within my study of technological capability I have been able to examine only a small number of the characteristics of a complex model. There is still a great deal of work yet to be done in defining the remaining characteristics within the model and identifying them in the classroom. Once this has been achieved, a more complete picture of the model can be created. Design and Technology in the National Curriculum is still developing and teachers are developing new strategies for shaping this.

The study I undertook had two main purposes: to find evidence for some of the characteristics and, second, to determine quite how pupils use an iterative process as they problem solve in technology. Broadly speaking, through the examination of children's dialogue, I felt it possible to identify some main characteristics within the model. I have to acknowledge that, as might be expected, I found more evidence to support some of the characteristics than others and, again as might be expected, on more than one occasion a single extract of dialogue could be used as evidence to identify more than one characteristic. This perhaps reinforces the idea of the interdependence of the characteristics within the model. They are thoroughly intertwined and should not be seen as isolated qualities.

The model does suggest that these characteristics are developed within an iterative process. Although there were some occasions when this could be said to be the case, it is perhaps impossible to say – with real conviction – that the 'holistic' picture of the design process can fully be represented as an iterative model. The work in these schools was, by and large, divided into free-standing sections. Within each section the iterative process could be glimpsed but there was little evidence that showed the overall growth of the process, developing and continuing throughout the entire body of work. Figure 2.2 is an attempt to show the how these short, repetitive, iterative activities were seen in the schools and how they might be developed to come some way closer to the original model.

It has become clear throughout the study that in order for the iterative process to develop the pupils need to acquire knowledge that they can then apply. It is not enough to rely on the pupils' own

Repetition of the isolated activities showing no
development in the iterative process

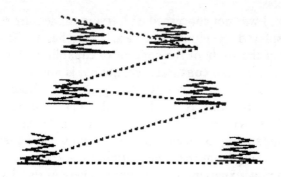

SEPARATE ACTIVITIES THAT EACH INVOLVE
THE ITERATIVE PROCESS LEADING TO OVERALL
DEVELOPMENT OF THE STYALISED TRIANGLE

Figure 2.2   Representation of the iterative process as observed in the pupils
working and suggested development

'possible acquisition' of knowledge. This in turn has implications for
the role of teachers, as to when they intervene in the design process –
either to present or direct the pupil to new information or to
encourage the pupil to be reflexive and questioning about their own
ideas as they evolve. I feel it is important to stress that new
information is not seen as 'chunks of knowledge' that the pupil is given
at regular intervals but, rather, that it is introduced or taught at a
relevant stage in the process through a child-centred and pupil-active
approach. This combination of teacher direction and pupil investigation may then go some way to overcoming the problems I saw of
pupils repeating the same, or similar ideas, making contrived decisions
based on limited criteria, all of which ultimately affected the realism of
their work.

There is no doubt that in both schools there was evidence of
valuable learning experience taking place. What the research shows is
that teachers must not only have a clear notion of the characteristics

that they wish the pupils to acquire, but must also posses the techniques to use in order to achieve this. Perhaps the important strategy here is to balance the structured input of information at the right time, and then allow sufficient flexibility for individual growth and the development of ideas.

There is undoubtedly a need for further work on the iterative process and how pupils use it. It is also necessary to consider just how the delivery and teaching of the technology might itself effect the iterative process.

In my work, I was not concerned with trying to measure the **level** of capability displayed by pupils, but clearly this has to be a natural development of the study of the concept of capability. Once teachers have indicators for what constitutes capability, is not the next step to find ways to define or quantify the quality of those identified capabilities? To me this is fundamental work that needs to be explored. Unless there are firm foundations to enable teachers to have a clear understanding of what they are trying to achieve – and everyone is working from the same definitions – then the arguments and dissatisfaction experienced by many teachers in the first years of the National Curriculum Technology will continue to rage. The model I have outlined should not be seen as restrictive, but one that sets a framework to give teachers confidence and direction, one that fosters stimulating, developmental work, through which the pupils' capability can grow and solve problems.

SECTION TWO

Extending contexts

This section describes the use of problem solving in three stimulating and varied contexts

CHAPTER THREE

Complex tales: small solutions. Problem solving in intermediate technology

Catherine Budgett-Meakin, Intermediate Technology Group

This chapter will explore a particular approach – appropriate technology – to problem solving, using 'Tales' from overseas which draw attention to parallels with contexts in Europe. These Tales prompt critical questioning of the role of technology in society, and the part it plays in encouraging or discouraging sustainability.

Sustainable development is usually defined as 'development that meets the needs of the present without compromising the ability of future generations to meet their own needs' (Schumaker, 1972). 'Development' is not, of course, only to do with the Third World. Development takes place all over the world, and much of it is unsustainable. In this chapter I shall refer to sustainability, rather than sustainable development, to remind ourselves of the global challenge presented.

First, what is the appropriate technology approach? In brief, it is an approach which has at its centre the needs of people and the environment. That means that any technology can be held up to the 'criteria' for an appropriate technology and measured against them. These criteria can be summarised as:

- Using local skills, and materials as much as possible;
- Using renewable sources of energy as much as possible;
- Damaging the environment as little as possible;
- Building sustainability into the outcome;
- Working with people in order to come up with environmentally sound solutions which meet their needs.

These criteria are not set in tablets of stone but provide useful parameters for examining technologies. Four aspects need to be introduced at this stage:

45

46

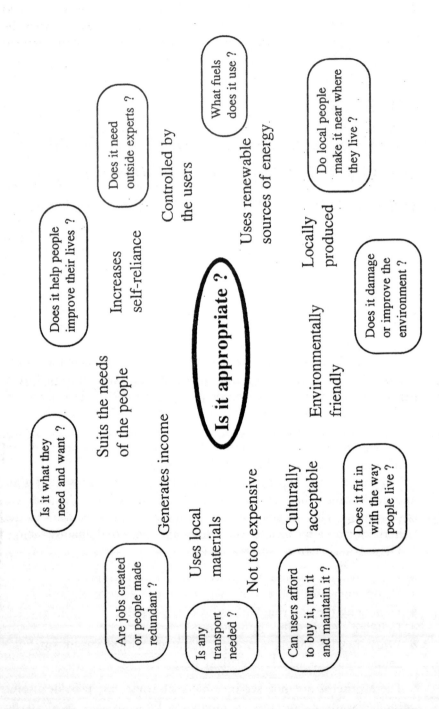

Figure 3.1

1. *The 'appropriate technology'* (AT) approach embraces broad issues: it is not simply a matter of **bits** of technology – indeed the 1990 National Curriculum document (DES, 1990) defined technology as 'an artefact, system or environment', which is a useful and familar place to start. One crucial element of the AT approach is the need to draw in disciplines other than those to do with technology and engineering – economics, anthropology and science. In educational terms this means that there is an opportunity to involve other departments – Geography, History, Religious Education and Science, for example.

2. *This book is concerned with 'Problem Solving in Science and Technology'.* The development of appropriate technologies and the broad-based approach indicated above have largely occurred in the so-called 'Third World'. There is a widespread belief that the 'Third World' is a **problem**; it is therefore quite easy to make a semantic switch and think that dealing with appropriate technologies is to do with 'solving Third World Problems'. As will be described below, this is inaccurate and unhelpful, and reinforces the omnipresent belief that the 'Third World' is passively waiting for the 'First World' to 'solve its problems'. The truth is somewhat different. Technology educators need to be aware of this potential confusion so that they do not risk their pupils thinking that they, the pupils, are trying to 'solve Third World problems'. To allow such a misinterpretation to persist would endorse the belief of racial superiority evident in many of our pupils.

3. *Terminology*: 25% of the world's population live in the 'First World', and consume 75% of the world's resources. The Education Office of Intermediate Technology, who have developed educational materials based on IT's project work, offers an alternative terminology to Third World/developing countries and First World/developed countires – Majority World and Minority World. These terms will be used from now on in this chapter. I need to say here that Intermediate Technology (IT) is an international development agency (a charity) working mainly in seven countries around the world. Founded in 1965 by E.F. Schumacher (the author of 'Small is Beautiful'), IT has offices in Peru, Sudan, Kenya, Zimbabwe, Sri Lanka and Bangladesh, each managed by local nationals. Project activities range from small-scale food processing to small-scale electricity generation, work with potters, animal health carers, food producers, textile workers, carpenters and house builders.

4. *Economics* – At the moment the world is driven by an economic system which benefits the countries of the Minority World and impoverishes the countries of the Majority World. We are constantly bombarded with television images from the Majority World of desperation and dependency: what we, the general public of the Minority World, are largely unaware of is the larger picture.

This is not the place to go into this in detail – for further reading see the suggested references at the end of the chapter. But it is worth quoting Schumacher (1972) who said 'the main content of politics is economics, and the main content of economics is technology'. For technology educators it is important to realise the inter-relatedness and interdependence of technology and economics. Indeed the 'Tales' that follow illustrate that point well.

To return to the issue of 'problems': clearly there are practical problems to be solved, all over the world, but usually that is the easy part. What is much harder is understanding the 'problem' in its wider context – cultural, environmental and economic. Schumacher said, back in 1972, that:

'the problem passengers on Space Ship Earth are the First Class passengers and no one else'.

By that he meant that the resource consumption and environmental pollution were largely carried out by the population of the Minority World – his 'first class passengers'. The technologist and the economist (and the technology educator) have an important role to play in tackling over-consumption and materialistic values.

As to problem solving in an educational context, the appropriate technology approach is useful as it concentrates on an open-ended approach, in which wide ranging discussion may lead to a variety of possible outcomes, and it may be that the original perceived 'problem' is not the real problem at all. 'The Woman's Tale', below, illustrates this point well.

It is now time to move on to the Tales.

The Cook's tale

Cooks constitute the second largest occupational group in the world (farmers are the largest). Cooks deal with technologies all the time, whether in the equipment they use, or the food technological knowledge they possess. But they are not often credited with being technologists, perhaps because they tend to be women, and because they rarely have economic power. Their knowledge is undervalued, and often, particularly in the Majority World, the cooking area is given little attention, and the equipment may be rudimentary.

All over the world the life of any household revolves around the preparation of meals. The most common means for cooking food in the Majority World is over a three stone fire, using wood as the fuel. Simple, portable and cheap, the fire provides a warm focus for the family, and the smoke has some beneficial effects: it keeps away insects, and can be used for smoking food to preserve it. But there are negative aspects. The fire is not energy efficient – fuel is expensive (particularly in urban areas) and often scarce. Collecting firewood is a time-consuming and arduous task. The smoke produced is hugely damaging to health.

The response to the need for energy-efficiency varies around the world. In the Minority World a pressure cooker is one energy-efficient answer. In many places ceramic energy-efficient stoves have been developed: the Anagi (which means excellent) in Sri Lanka; the Upesi (which means swift) in Kenya, and heat storage cookers developed in Nepal.

In West Kenya a stoves project began in 1989, training groups of women potters to make and market ceramic Upesi stove-liners, which are built into the house and coated with mud to add insulation, and therefore fuel efficiency and durability. One group produces between 500 and 1000 good quality liners per month, providing not only the cook with a useful product, but also generating much needed income for the stove makers (Figure 3.2).

In Nepal the countless rivers and streams which fall from the Himalayas provide Nepal with its greatest resource. For centuries people living in the mountains have harnessed this resource to process their crops, using water mills called pani ghattas. During the last 30 years, work has taken place to introduce steel water turbines made in Nepal which generate electricity (micro hydro) for remote villages. This is an absorbing story, with many messages for the Minority World (see *The Farmer's Tale*) but here we must focus on the relevance for the Cook.

One spin-off benefit of available electricity was the potential to use the energy for cooking. The concept of heat storage cooking came from a technical analysis of how energy could be stored in off-peak periods (similar to storage heaters in the UK) and released for cooking as required: the actual development of the cooker was led by an understanding of the needs and desires of the eventual users of the cooker.

Figure 3.2 Cooking at the Upesi stove, Kenya

Several prototype cookers have been developed and tested by villagers, with modifications being introduced as a result of the Cook's comments and criticisms. What became clear is that social, economic and cultural factors are inseparable from technical work in the design of cookers. The success of such a technology, measured in terms of the benefits to the user depends on the level of understanding of these issues by the designer, and the extent to which the designers permit the views of the eventual users to inform the design process.

It is important to remember that it is the Minority World that consumes energy greedily, as if there were no tomorrow. There is a mistaken belief that it is the peoples of the Majority World that are the energy vandals: the Majority World with 75% of the world's population uses 16% of the energy resources. It should therefore be the Minority World that should be tackling energy consumption seriously – and what better place to start than the domestic kitchen!

The Gardener's Tale

Recently Zimbabwe has emerged from a devastating drought which lasted for 4 years. Conservation and husbanding of scarce water therefore became essential. South West of Harare is Chivi district where there is a long tradition of gardening for growing food crops. Working with the local community, it became clear, through discussions, that the most pressing need was for ways to conserve water. The women are already familiar with pottery skills: what has been developed is an elegant, simple and sustainable solution which is catching on fast. Clay pipes are shaped round a wet roller, and held in a slit open PVC drainpipe to get the shape right. The PVC pipe can then be removed. After 2 days of air drying, the pipes are fired in a local kiln and then joined together. A curved angle is attached at one end, with an upward slanting section. The pipe is then laid into the soil, at a depth of approximately 15 cm (6 in). The end under the soil is closed off, the pipe is covered with soil, and filled with water through the slanting section which remains above the ground.

Because the clay is porous, and the joins between the sections not completely water-tight, the water seeps out at the level of the roots of the lines of plants, delivering a slow and consistent supply of water to the plant (Figure 3.3).

It looks as though water savings of up to 33% can be achieved, and as much as 50% can be conserved. Now Mrs Mlambo, the Gardener of this Tale, only has to water her garden once or twice a week. She is now successfully growing tomatoes, onions and a leaf vegetable type of rape.

This is a good example of 'technology transfer'. Usually this term is understood to mean 'technology being transferred from the Minority World to the Majority World': this water conservation idea came from India, and is an excellent example of sustainable and appropriate technology. Local knowledge and skills are being used, and members of the community have been closely involved in identifying their own problems and in solving them themselves.

The Farmer's Tale

High up in the Yorkshire Dales, just as in Nepal, some farms are not on the National Grid. The source of electricity has been an expensive and noisy diesel generator. The farmer and his wife, Bill and Ann Cowperthwaite, were offered the chance of a micro-hydro system that would provide them with a sustainable source of power. Luckily they have a healthy stream which provides enough energy to power an innovative generating system which comprises, in effect, running three electrical water pumps in reverse. The falling of rain is now warmly welcomed, as it secures the electricity for the farmhouse. The family have become experts in knowing how to balance the load on the

Figure 3.3 A gardener watering crop through a clay pipe, Zimbabwe

turbine – as Ann said 'most women count calories – I count kilowatts!' (Figure 3.4).

This is a clear example of an appropriate technology being adapted for use in the Minority World.

The Woman's Tale

This Tale may seem out of place to readers, but it has a useful message. All women, all over the world, menstruate. How that is dealt with depends on cultural and religious customs. It would probably be appropriate to hazard a guess that everywhere, to a greater or lesser extent, menstruation is a matter of shame or at least embarrassment. In many cultures, including our own, there is distaste about something which is entirely natural, and which is indeed a sign of fertility and health.

Until fairly recently (in this century in Europe) the technology for dealing with the flow of blood was, in effect, napkins which were washed out and re-used. Nothing wrong with that, and in fact there is a move to return to reusable sanitary protection, because of the environmental implications of disposal. Some of the same arguments are now being used about disposable babies' nappies.

The technological development in the Minority World was initially sanitary towels, followed by tampons. Tampons largely deny the issue of menstruation as the 'problem' is kept out of sight.

Taboos about menstruation are widespread, and particularly so in a Muslim country like Bangladesh, where women are dominated by men. A study into menstrual practices revealed that the health of women was jeopardised by the custom of using and re-using rags that were not allowed to see the light of day, and were therefore harbingers of germs and disease. The rags are washed out and then secreted under beds, where they do not get a chance to dry properly. The solution to this problem was not to introduce either disposable or reusable sanitary protection, because of the costs, but to tackle the public education and public hygiene issues.

A campaign is now being run to inform both men and women about the naturalness of menstruation and the threat to health associated with menstruation practices. Changing deeply entrenched social attitudes is a long-term business, which cannot happen quickly (other examples might be bandaging up children's feet in China, clitoridectomy in the Arab world and sending small children up chimneys and down mines in England).

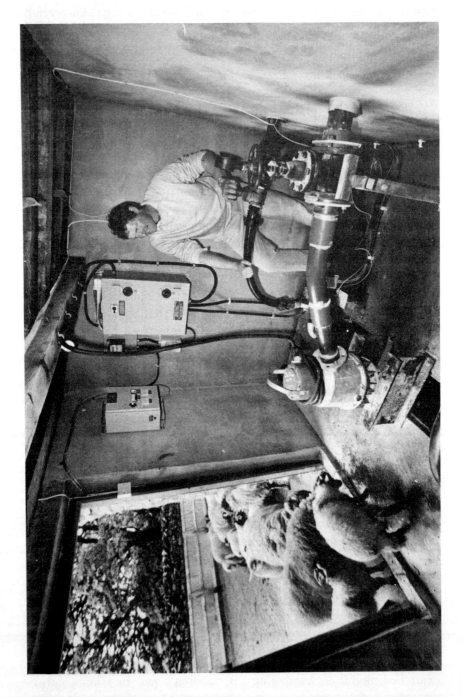

Figure 3.4 The farmer in his turbine house, UK (Reproduced with kind permission of the *Guardian*)

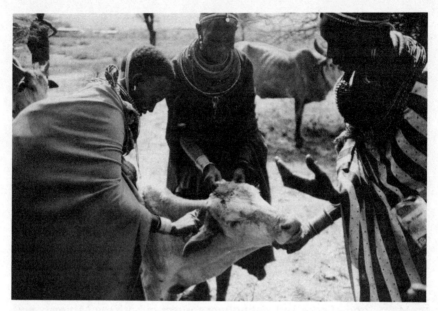

Figure 3.5 Animal health trainees applying tick grease, Kenya

So what appears to be a technical problem is in fact one of attitudes and culture.

The Vet's Tale

Knowledge and the sharing of ideas is the currency of human development. People have a right to know what is known. In an ideal world, knowledge should be presented in context with balanced guidance as to the implications of the use of the knowledge. Problems arise when the knowledge is given false value and when it is applied partially and perhaps illogically. Status is often given to a particular technological solution, even though the solution is entirely inappropriate.

Ticks and tick-borne diseases are among the more important animal health problems of pastoralists in northern Kenya. Modern research into the control of ticks has focused on large-scale settled farms: the usual way of dealing with the problem is dipping. Such methods are inappropriate in nomadic areas, where the local breeds have much greater natural immunity to the ticks and the diseases they carry: regular dipping can interfere with this immunity and make the animals more susceptible to disease. The cost of dipping is also prohibitive.

So, what is appropriate ? It is not yet clear what is the best way to use knowledge for the benefit of nomadic people. So far the way forward has been to assess the enormous fund of indigenous knowledge about ticks. The challenge is to find the best ways for the farmers to get at the information which is most useful for them. Information is power: it enables choices to be made and alternatives to be assessed (Figure 3.5).

The Trainer's Tale

Food processing on a small scale provides an important source of income for people all over the world: it is the rationale for processing food. But too often training has focused on the technical aspects of food hygiene while forgetting the marketing and business aspects. Whether you are selling pots of marmalade in a farm shop, ice cream from a van, or snack foods on the streets of Bangladesh, if you have not got your packaging, promotion and marketing plan together, you will not sell your product.

Many food science and technology courses in both the Minority and Majority Worlds do not include entrepreneurial training, and most focus on large-scale sophisticated technologies that are inappropriate to the needs of small-scale producers. Intermediate Technology has developed a series of independent, linked modules that can be slotted together to provide a flexible tailor-made training package for the trainee.

The really novel features of the training are the approach to practical food production and the integration of technical and business aspects when studying each food process. Role-plays and simulations are used to make the training come alive, with all participants having the opportunity to be 'managers' at some point. The 'manager' is responsible for organising all aspects of production to meet a purchase order. This Tale illustrates the close interdependence of technology, science and business studies.

A Tale worth its Salt

This is a Tale about women in Sierra Leone who extract salt from silt and prepare it for sale in markets. Salt is a commodity valued in almost all societies – for its preserving and taste-enhancing qualities. Our word 'salary' comes from the Latin word for salt.

Using their scientific knowledge and technological skills, women were able to develop the salt extraction technology from the simple method of boiling sea water to brine, and finally to the sophisticated and more efficient salt-from-silt technique. They displayed remarkable knowledge of scientific principles, and imagination in their technological approach. In their effort to introduce innovations to existing technologies, women transferred and adapted techniques from other areas of production, such as the use of perforated soap-making baskets for salt extraction.

In addition to developing more productive filtration methods, the women undertook marketing initiatives so that salt became one of the major sources of cash income for many rural women in Sierra Leone.

Such a story tackles both gender and 'Third World' stereotypes.

Principles and issues

What principles and issues emerge from these Tales?

1. The real and most important issue is not necessarily the one that presents itself at first glance.
2. Cultural and environmental factors need to be taken into consideration.
3. Politics and economics are inextricably linked with technology.
4. It is often inappropriate to try and solve someone else's problem without involving the users as the primary source of information.
5. The satisfaction of human need is paramount.
6. Technology has an important role in either threatening or enhancing sustainability: and the appropriate technology approach has much to teach us about the sustainable aspects of technologies.
7. Women are rarely considered as 'technologists', though indeed they are concerned with technology in many areas of their lives.
8. A simple and elegant solution to a problem takes real imagination. As Schumacher said 'Any third-rate engineer can make a complicated apparatus more complicated, but it takes a touch of genius to find one's way back to principles'.

So what is the relevance of all these Tales for teachers and education? There is ample evidence to support the case for using case studies to illustrate particular points. The requirement to examine technologies from 'different cultures' does mean that it is necessary to have authoritative resources on which to draw.

A recently published IT Education Pack – *Creating Art, Creating Income* – focuses on a Women's Textile Co-operative in Bangladesh.

It was trialled in a school in Chiswick. The slides described the context, and a second set of slides, shown at the time of project evaluation, of actual products amazed the pupils by their intricacy and high quality. Comments by pupils from their final evaluation included: 'I wish all our projects were as exciting as this one' and 'It's a pity we didn't have more time'. The pupils grasped that they were not 'solving the problems of others' but were acknowledging and appreciating some of the economic, cultural and technological constraints. They achieved some level of empathy and understanding of wider issues, while meeting the demands of the National Curriculum.

There is a good deal of concern about the importance of values in technology education. The whole nature of 'problem solving' requires that such issues are tackled. Who wins and who loses are questions that pupils and their teachers need to consider in the context of technology education, and the alternative technology approach lends itself to such an examination.

It is important to realise the relevance of the appropriate technology approach for the Minority World, quite as much as for the Majority World. Although technology cannot be divorced from the economic system of which it is a part, we would do well to examine the technologies with which we are surrounded, and to ask critical questions about their role in making a future that works for all of us, rich and poor. *Small is Beautiful*, Schumacher's book (1972), had the subtitle 'Economics as if People mattered'. He also coined the phrase 'technology with a human face'.

If we are concerned about the future of the planet, we need constantly to remind ourselves that 80% of the damage to the environment is being carried out by the Minority World, through the inappropriate use of technology. As educators, however, we must be careful not to load ourselves and our pupils with guilt and feelings of powerlessness. We can do something to change the way we live our lives, and to the way we use and view technologies.

We need to ask about wants and needs in relation to technologies. These issues are explored further in Budgett-Meakin (1992) and in that book are a multitude of classroom ideas about how to adopt a new view of both the world and technology.

Bearing in mind the second 'aspect' mentioned at the beginning of this chapter – that 'solving problems' is not about 'solving Third World problems' – contexts using the alternative technology approach must be found within our own society. These might involve environmentally sound practices at school and home, sustainable technology transport solutions, and energy options that focus on renewable sources of energy – see Chapters 7 and 8 of my *Make the Future Work* (Budgett-Meakin, 1992), and Edwards, Watts and West (1993) (*Making the Difference*). The Tales in this chapter might then be used to illustrate a particular point and to provide starting points for more lateral thinking in the workshop or classroom. Other booklets – such as *Strategies and Guidelines* – aim to support teachers as they embark on tackling development and environment issues in their educational work. A full educational resource list is available from the IT Education Office, Intermediate Technology, Myson House, Railway Terrace, Rugby CV21 3HT.

Conclusion

This chapter has introduced a global view of 'problem solving'. By introducing the appropriate technology approach, reference has been made to the sustainable uses of technology, and to the responsibility of technology educators to introduce such perspectives to their teaching.

CHAPTER FOUR

Problem solving – the industrial context

Bill Harrison, Sheffield Hallam University

Why introduce the industrial context into the science and technology curriculum?

For the purpose of this chapter '*industry*' is used to include manufacturing, service industries, retail, financial, commercial, leisure, agriculture, public sector organisations, etc. It covers the multinational company as well as the small garage and corner shop. Too often industry is incorrectly thought of as being only associated with manufacturing and engineering, which of course is to severely limit its usefulness as a context for the curriculum.

Although school-industry collaboration is not a recent phenomenon, it was particularly intensified during Industry Year (1986). Business involvement with schools was then further encouraged as a result of CBI and government initiatives. This activity also happened to coincide with changes in the science curriculum to include industrial, technological, social and economic issues in science courses. So, with pressure for change coming from both directions it was not surprising to see so much growth in schools-industry developments since the mid 1980s. It is not appropriate here to trace these developments, but readers wishing to do so are referred, for example, to Chapter 2 in *Open Chemistry* (Harrison and Ramsden, 1992).

What is important to consider here are the benefits of introducing the industrial context into the science and technology curriculum. Some of the key advantages are given below:

- It provides an enormous range of real and relevant contexts for learning about science and technology and the likelihood of increased motivation.
- Students gain a much wider understanding and appreciation of

the role of science and technology in their lives, and facts and principles are not divorced from the social, economic, environmental aspects.

● It provides excellent opportunities for introducing aspects of the cross-curricular themes, e.g. economic and industrial understanding, environmental, health and careers education thus enabling students and teachers to better understand and appreciate the world of business and education.

● It provides mutual support structures and strategies, e.g. for placements, visits, visitors, curriculum development, training courses, careers work, project work, etc. and promotes valuable partnerships between education and business.

Why is problem solving a particularly useful strategy for introducing the industrial context and vice versa?

One only has to talk to industrialists to realise the importance industry places on problem solving, decision making and achieving results for a specific purpose. Indeed it could be argued that successful business is essentially about solving problems effectively and efficiently.

Industry, therefore, provides an almost endless range of realistic and relevant problems on which to base stimulating activities for science and technology courses. Of course it is not always possible to use a problem directly, but with some adaptation and manipulation by the teacher and the participating company it is usually possible to produce an effective resource.

In addition, by involving industrialists in the curriculum development process it enables the school to benefit not only from their technical expertise, but often from the company's expertise in problem solving.

Participating in problem solving with industry can enable children to value their own problem-solving capability. It can also teach them the importance of approaching problems systematically and using all the resources of the team.

What problem-solving resources and initiatives are already available?

There are now a significant number of good examples of problem-solving materials for science and technology involving industrial issues and applications. One of the early examples of such material was developed in the 1970s by the Chemistry Department at Glasgow University in collaboration with the Scottish Education Department (ICTP, 1977). Sixteen interactive learning packages were produced which covered a wide range of topics highlighting the social, industrial, economic and technological aspects of chemistry for O-grade/O-level students. The packages included small group discussion, simulation, and problem-solving or decision-making strategies.

Several units form the innovative project *Experimenting with Industry*, established by the Standing Conference on School Science and Technology with the ASE in 1985, also included problem-solving activities. Thirteen units were produced by the project, covering a wide range of school practical work based on industrial applications, as a result of linking the teacher-writers with industrial companies.

The *SATIS (Science and Technology in Society)* project published the first 70 units in 1986. Many of these, including further units produced during the late 1980s and early 1990s, were developed in collaboration with industry and included several problem-solving activities.

The *Teaching Strategies in Biotechnology Project*, published in 1987, funded through TRIST and later the Training Agency and based at Sheffield University, also included several problem-solving simulation/role-play activities set in an industrially related context, e.g. Vinegar Production and the Mini Fermenter.

Another problem-solving project of considerable importance is *PAST 16*, published in 1992 by the ASE and Employment Department. A wide range of problem-solving briefs, case studies and exemplars, together with a valuable problem solving method study guide was produced by teachers from Walsall and Staffordshire LEAs with some contributions from industrialists. The aim was to promote scientific and technological problem-solving approaches in programmes for 16–19 year olds. Many of the problems either deal with issues which have links with industry or strongly encourage students to make contact with industry to help with solutions. Very useful strategies adopted by the project for teaching problem solving will be highlighted in a later section.

Recently, however, three major curriculum development projects in science and technology have produced or are currently producing a wide range of problem-solving materials in collaboration with industry. It is worth describing these briefly, since they each place considerable emphasis on problem solving within an industrial context.

Problem Solving with Industry Project (PSI) (1990) is based at the

Centre for Science Education, Sheffield Hallam University. More than 20 science teachers and advisory teachers, each working in collaboration with a company, have developed problem-solving investigations based on realistic industrial problems or situations. The project pack contains 18 units produced in four booklets aimed at key stages 3 and 4 and is suitable for both science and technology courses. It is also of use with some post-16 courses. The teacher's guide provides some very helpful strategies for teaching problem solving and will be highlighted in a later section along with examples from the units.

The Exciting Science and Engineering project sponsored by BP and developed and published during 1991/92 at the Chemical Industry Education Centre, University of York includes many examples of problem-solving activities related to industrial applications and issues for 7–14 year olds. Teachers are encouraged and helped to identify a local engineer who can support them in using the materials and strategies in the classroom. An example from one of the 12 units is described later.

Science with Technology Project (1993) is a current joint initiative of the Association for Science Education and the Design and Technology Association. The aim of the project is to develop the relationship between science and technology for students aged 14–19 and to encourage co-operation between departments. The materials, which will support work in both subjects, will be matched to the requirements of the National Curriculum and GCSE in Science and Technology for KS4 and post-16 GNVQ as well as A/AS level. The project will enable students to acquire science skills and knowledge in a way that makes them useful in design and make tasks. Problem-solving tasks will be set in realist and relevant contexts, drawing whenever possible on a wide range of industrial contexts. Materials are currently being developed and trialled and the first set of units will be available later this year. An example from the trial units will be described.

Before finishing this section it is worth drawing attention to two closely related innovative initiatives centred around problem solving with industry. Both projects were initiated and organised by a tertiary college and involved staff, students, pupils from local schools and local industrialists working together on real industrial problems. The problems were actual problems presented by the companies for pupils to solve at an event or over a period of several days. The projects had a number of key aims but two important ones were to show the relevance of science and technology in the work-place, and to improve student and pupil images of science, technology and engineering industries, and the world of work generally, through collaborative problem solving. The first of these projects, *Health Matters*, was initiated and organised by Wilberforce sixth-Form College in Hull in 1990 and brought together over 1000 year 9 pupils and around 50 companies to solve health-related problems. The second, the *Cluster Links* project, was initiated and organised by staff at Castle Tertiary College in Sheffield in 1992 and involved over 300 school children and college students and 30 local companies, successfully solving over 30 problems. All pupils and students visited the work-place at least once, some spent 4 days there. The project was linked to the CREST award scheme. It was modelled closely on the Hull project and will be repeated again in 1993. Figure 4.1 shows a pupil design brief from the Health Matters project produced in collaboration with Northern Foods.

Strategies for developing problem solving in partnership with industry

Teacher secondments/Industrialist secondments

Unfortunately long secondments of teachers into industry of up to a year, such as those which were offered by ICI, are relatively uncommon, but of course were very effective. However, even 3 or 4 days, if well planned and structured, can be used to considerable effect, e.g. as in the *Experimenting with Industry Project* and the *Problem Solving with Industry Project.*

Many teachers have benefited considerably from the UBI *Teacher Placement Service* (1991), usually operated by the Education Business Partnerships with funding from the Training and Enterprise Councils. Teachers generally spend up to one week in industry, during which time they could identify and develop activities and resources for work back in the classroom.

There are also cases where industrialists are seconded to schools, and this can open up a host of opportunities for curriculum development whilst providing excellent access to the company and its resources.

Visits and visitors

A short visit by the teacher to a company can generate ideas for problems, provide information, data, leaflets for use in developing

Food in the kitchen

Food poisoning happens because harmful bacteria get onto food. Northern Foods is a large company producing many different food items. When someone gets food poisoning an investigation takes place. Very often the food poisoning bacteria are found in the kitchen, not in the factory.

Northern Foods want to get the message across to people at home that they must prepare food carefully.

Brief

Design a leaflet which Northern Foods could send into homes about food safety.

Points you will need to think about:

1. How do bacteria get onto food?

2. Where do the food poisoning bacteria come from?

3. How can people prepare food safely?

4. What information do you want to put into your leaflet?

5. How will you make sure it is read?

Problem 2

Figure 4.1 A pupil design brief from the *Health Matters Project*

resources for lessons, help in planning an effective visit by pupils or simply make valuable contacts for future work.

Using industrial visitors to the classroom can be a very powerful resource, particularly if the students themselves take responsibility for planning, organising and running the session. The visitor, as well as being an information source, e.g. in providing background information or setting the scene for a problem-solving investigation or simulation, can also take an active role as facilitator, chairman or observer/reporter. An industrial visit by a class of students can be a very valuable and motivating learning experience, particularly when it is planned to complement current work in school or college. It is ideally suited to supporting problem solving work by reinforcing the realism and relevance, crucial to student motivation and involvement.

Whether or not a visit or visitor is being used to enrich the learning, both strategies require good planning. Readers wishing for more detailed advice are referred to the chapter on using visits and visitors in *Active Teaching and Learning Approaches in Science* (1992) also the section dealing with structured industrial visits in the *Chemistry for Science Teachers Project*, theme 5 – The Environment (1992).

Company literature or documents

Most larger companies provide literature either for general use or in some cases designed specifically for schools. In the former case it is often possible to use the material directly or adapt it for classroom use (Harrison and Nicholson, 1993). In any case, the injection of this type of resource brings an extra dimension and greater sense of realism to the learning experience and can be particularly useful as necessary background information in problem-solving activities.

Business – Education Support Agencies

There are several agencies able to offer support to teachers wishing to make contact with industry or to introduce an industrial dimension into their teaching.

SATRO (Science and Technology Regional Organisation) has a long record of successfully bringing schools and industry together and for promoting better understanding of the applciations of science and technology.

Regional Education – Business Partnerships (EBPs) are oganisations created to bring the worlds of education and business closer together and would normally embrace activities such as work experience, Compact, Teacher Placement Scheme, whilst working alongside LEA officers, Careers Service, teachers and industrialists.

Schools Curriculum and Industry Partnership (SCIP) is a national education/industry organisation, with a regional network of over 120 LEA based co-ordinators, who work with teachers and industrialists to give the school curriculum an industrial dimension. SCIPSIMS (1991) and *Good Ideas for EIU* (1992) are two series of exercises, some involving problem solving and decision making, which have been developed by SCIP in partnership with teachers and industrialists.

Teaching problem solving using the industrial context

Problem solving can perhaps be considered as the most powerful of all the commonly regarded active learning strategies. It can certainly be seen as an over-arching strategy which will often involve small group discussion, role play, simulation, active reading and writing, presentation, group investigations, data handling, etc. However, it is a strategy commonly perceived by teachers as being time consuming. Although most agree that a broad range of valuable skills are being developed, the pressures they feel on them to cover the large amount of subject content are such that unless the activity specifically targets that subject knowledge and understanding, it is unlikely to be used.

The challenge therefore, to curriculum developers, is to produce problem-solving experiences for students which closely target the subject topic knowledge and understanding and which do not take up an excessive amount of curriculum time. This is made even more difficult when the industrial context or an applications-first rather than a sicence-first approach is adopted. This is because problems based on applications of science do not normally fall neatly under one syllabus heading and indeed several concepts/principles may be introduced within the problem at any one time. Harrison and Ramsden (1992) have identified some of the problems of using an application-first approach which are outlined below:

● When several concepts are being introduced each is unlikely to be given adequate coverage and, if a new concept, would need to be returned to at another time.
● It may impose an order of teaching which is considered inappropriate.
● It is often difficult and time consuming to design practical work which simulates or mirrors the industrial application.

- Time and effort are required to assemble resources, in some cases to liaise with industry, and to possibly update the teacher's own knowledge and understanding of the industrial application or issue.

The authors also, of course, identified several important benefits in using an industrial context or applications-first approach and these have been outlined in the first section of this chapter. Harrison and Ramsden go on to state that, despite the growing amount of industrially-related material available and the greater involvement and support of industry in curriculum development, there has been a limited take-up of the applications-first approach in school chemistry. (This can be equally applied to school science generally.) They believe that although many teachers fully accept the value of this approach, the demands of developing and using these materials, particularly at a time of major curriculum change, are just too much. Also, many teachers may not be ready or even willing to make a change which is radically different to the generally accepted pedagogy of (science) teaching. However, attempts have been made to develop problem-solving materials in science and technology which do aim to cover specific syllabus content. Some examples from several projects are now described, along with some of the approaches to problem solving and the strategies used to teach it.

The Problem Solving with Industry project (PSI), based at Sheffield Hallam University, has used a variety of real and relevant problems, set in a wide range of industrial contexts, in order to cover science and technology content and processes along with aspects of the cross-curricular themes of economic and industrial understanding, environmental education and health education. This is illustrated in Figure 4.2.

The PSI project uses a four stage model to describe the problem-solving process. This general problem-solving model can be related (Figure 4.3) to the three strands for Scientific Investigations and the four Attainment Targets for design and technology capability in the respective National Curriculum documents.

These 'processes' or models do not infer that students simply follow a converging path towards a solution. Creativity, imagination and intuition are important qualities in problem solving, but a more structured approach can order thinking without stifling these qualities. Providing a system or structured approach is more likely to help the problem solver reach a more speedy and satisfactory result, as well as developing a method of working that can be used repeatedly in new situations (PSI, 1990).

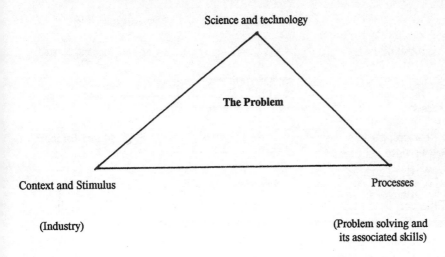

Figure 4.2 The problem: providing the context, content and process

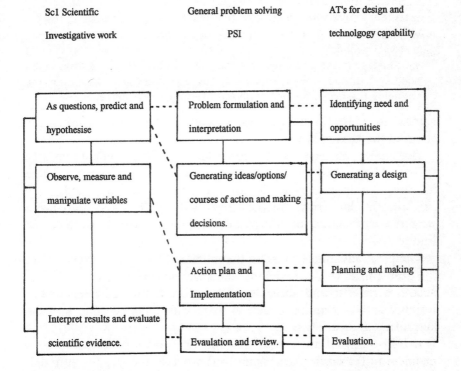

Figure 4.3 Relationship between scientific investigation, design and technology capability 'processes' and the PSI general problem-solving model

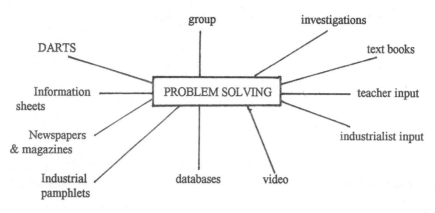

Figure 4.4 Information from various sources to solve a problem

Support for a structured approach to problem solving, particularly with respect to the industrial context is reinforced by Chambers (1989), when she states:

'structured problem-solving approaches are used in industry because they can often provide the most effective means of getting desired results. Making connections between the process of getting results and solving problems in industry and similar processes in teaching and learning can open up significant questions about the nature of the teacher's task. It can help to provide a framework for conscious reflection which can support the beginning teacher in his or her own professional development.'

Further details of the structured approach advocated by Chambers are given in the next section.

One important aspect of problem solving is that students have to gather, evaluate and use information from a variety of sources. These include written materials, graphs and tables, surveys and, very importantly, data from practical investigations. The PSI units use a wide range of sources of information for students to use, as shown in Figure 4.4.

The great advantage of using the industrial context in which to set the problem, as well as involving industrial personnel, is of course the access to realistic and accurate information. It may be necessary to simplify data or simulate practical work which can be done with the help of the industrialist.

It is also important to note that practical investigations may be a means of gathering data from one source only, and although extremely valuable, may be simply one component of a more holistic view of problem solving. It is therefore very important that students have experience of problem solving in science lessons which goes beyond the controlling variables and fair testing model of scientific investigations, not least because the latter offers a too narrow view of scientific problem solving and indeed, the way that scientific research is undertaken.

Yet another advantage found by the PSI project in using the industrial context for problem solving, is that students begin to appreciate the importance of problem solving as a means of achieving results for a purpose, rather than simply as a means of solving an interesting or challenging puzzle. With the emphasis on getting results and achievement, problem solving can be viewed in a much more positive light, in which problems become *opportunities* for achieving success. This view of problem solving has been promoted by the Comino Foundation's GRASP®* (Getting Results and Solving Problems) approach (1990). GRASP® stresses the importance of clearly defining purposes, and criteria for achieving success. Monitoring and control of the process by continuous checking and reviewing of actions against purposes and criteria for success are essential components of the GRASP® process.

The PSI project has found that when students are introduced to a structured approach to problem solving they can be helped in the beginning with strategies that enable them to cope more effectively with each stage of the process. The method is to use process planning sheets for each stage which act as a means of guiding students through the process without reducing their input. An example of such a prompt sheet is given in Figure 4.5.

Students quickly learn to cope without the support sheets but they are very helpful for students being introduced to problem solving. Students can start with structured problem solving exercises, perhaps working on specific tasks which give practice of particular stages, before moving on to more open-ended, holistic problems as their skill and confidence grows.

Other helpful strategies for enabling students to improve their skills at each stage of the problem solving process are given in the PSI teacher support manual. It is particularly important to remember that students often have difficulty at the first stage, i.e. problem formulation and interpretation, and need considerable practice to master this stage. They will have little chance of tackling the problem effectively if they have incorrectly formulated or interpreted it. This point is reinforced by Chambers (1989) when she stresses that:

*GRASP is a trademark of the Comino Foundation.

72

PS1   The Problem

Name   Group

Unit title

What is the problem and what are you trying to achieve?

Why is there a problem and a need to solve it?

What are all the different things that the problem depends on and
what do you need to find out about them?

What information and materials are available to help you solve it?

Figure 4.5 PSI Process Planning Sheet for problem formulation and identification stage

'the process of problem solving depends upon the process of problem
identification – what is it that we want to make happen? Why have we
chosen that particular aim? Schools are finding that industrial contexts can
provide superb opportunities for children to recognise for themselves the
importance of this aspect of problem solving. Companies are quite often
willing to pass on their initial formulation of a problem to a group of
children, who can go on to analyse the exact nature of the problem more
clearly.'

As mentioned earlier, it is important that the necessary subject
knowledge and understanding is covered as an integral part of the
problem-solving activity. There is likely to be more take-up by
teachers if problem solving is done 'in-place of' more traditional
methods of teaching in order to cover syllabus content, rather than as
an 'add on' done to give pupils experience of the problem-solving
process itself. It should not be seen as a peripheral activity. A key
objective of the PSI project was to try to ensure that the required

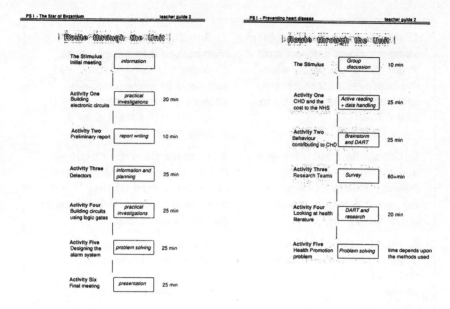

Figure 4.6 Approach used to integrate subject within the problem-solving process

science subject knowledge normally covered, would also be covered in the problem-solving activity within a similar time allocation. Whilst it was not always possible to achieve this, Figure 4.6 illustrates the approach used in two of the units.

Both of the above units start with a stimulus activity aimed to trigger the pupils' interest, to set the scene for the problem and to encourage them to want to take part enthusiastially. This is important in any teaching/learning activity, but particularly so in problem solving here the pupils are required to take more responsibility for their learning. So the need to get them involved and immersed in the problem right from the start is vital. The industrial context in itself can often provide the stimulus for involvement simply by presenting the pupils with realistic and relevant issues to address.

A range of different activities, such as DARTS (Directed Activities Related to Texts), data handling, small group discussion, brainstorming, survey and research work, short practical investigations and report writing are all used to provide background knowledge, both to undertake the problem successfully and to cover important subject content. These strategies are interwoven into the overall problem solving process.

The Exciting Science and Engineering project based at the

1. Introduction of the problem using a type of cartoon strip to get the pupils to consider the best way of transporting salt from a solution mine to a coal mine.	2. Small group work using a briefing sheet to get pupils to consider the information they will need to make a decision. They obtain their answers by questioning the teacher or a visiting engineer.
3. Group discussion following questioning, then decision making. This is followed by teacher-led discussion of group decisions.	4. A memo from the Chlorine Plant seeking help from pupils on how to speed up the dissolving process, introduced by the engineer or teacher.
5. Small group work to design simple experiments to test ideas, which are then carried out.	6. Pupils produce a written report of their findings in a memo to the company. Some groups report to whole class.
7. Engineer presents class with short series of questions to get pupils to consider the implications of their findings for a large scale process.	8. Activity concludes with a homework sheet '*To pump or Not to pump*' which contains questions on how the Cheshire Salt Corporation might measure brine concentration in its bore holes.

Figure 4.7 Stages in the unit: what's the problem

University of York illustrates very well in the unit *What's the Solution?* how a problem-solving activity set in an industrial context can be used to support key stage 3 science. Figure 4.7 gives a breakdown of the stages in the unit and Figure 4.8 shows how it could fit into a variety of syllabus topics.

The Yoghurt Project, a unit being developed for the *Science with Technology project*, is a good example of how National Curriculum science and technology subject content and economic and industrial understanding can be addressed by using a range of learning strategies set within the context of a real-life industrial problem-solving simulation. Figure 4.9 outlines the curriculum development process and teaching sequence for the unit.

The *PAST 16* project which advocates a structured approach to problem solving has developed a very useful model which draws on

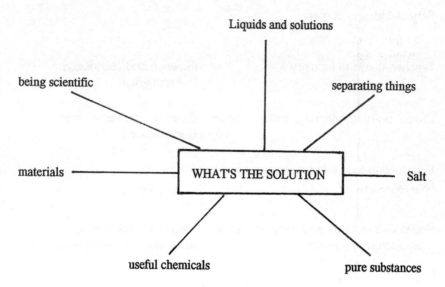

Figure 4.8 How the unit can support the teaching of a range of subjects

the work of DeBono (1978), Jackson (1983) and Instone (1988) and is illustrated in Figure 4.10.

The problem-solving briefs are presented to students in the form of action notes which provide ideas and suggestions for students to consider and do at each of the above stages. A self-evaluation sheet is provided with each brief so that students can review their work. The 25 action notes are very useful along with the 80 problems offered in the problem bank and the three case studies. Case Study 3 – 'Working with Industry' is particulary useful in that it shows the various ways in which a school can link with industry in real problem-solving activities. The teaching notes on problem solving are very helpful.

Finally, it is worth drawing attention to the INDTEL (Industry and Teacher Education Liaison) consortium materials – *Pathways to Partnership*, Module 5: 'Problem Solving with Industry' (1989) which has some interesting and valuable points to make about problem solving within an industrial context. Although the material is designed for student teachers, the aim is also to provide them with the models for classroom applications. Some useful strategies and activities are given for teaching students to approach problems in a systematic way. This approach, like the PSI project at Sheffield Hallam University, draws heavily on the GRASP® approach referred to earlier.

Module 5 consists of five units with activities aimed at developing problem-solving capability.

76

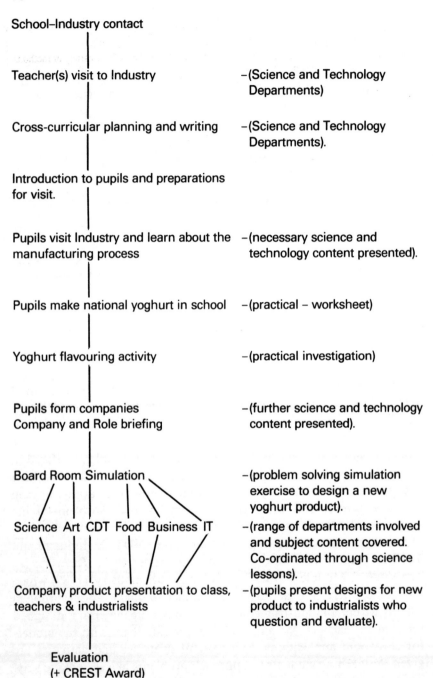

School–Industry contact

Teacher(s) visit to Industry   –(Science and Technology
                                        Departments)

Cross-curricular planning and writing   –(Science and Technology
                                         Departments).

Introduction to pupils and preparations
for visit.

Pupils visit Industry and learn about the –(necessary science and
manufacturing process   technology content presented).

Pupils make national yoghurt in school   –(practical – worksheet)

Yoghurt flavouring activity   –(practical investigation)

Pupils form companies   –(further science and technology
Company and Role briefing   content presented).

Board Room Simulation   –(problem solving simulation
                                     exercise to design a new
                                     yoghurt product).

Science Art CDT Food Business IT   –(range of departments involved
                                     and subject content covered.
                                     Co-ordinated through science
                                     lessons).
Company product presentation to class, –(pupils present designs for new
teachers & industrialists   product to industrialists who
                                     question and evaluate).

Evaluation
(+ CREST Award)

Figure 4.9 The Yoghurt Project Unit: Curriculum development process and teaching
sequence

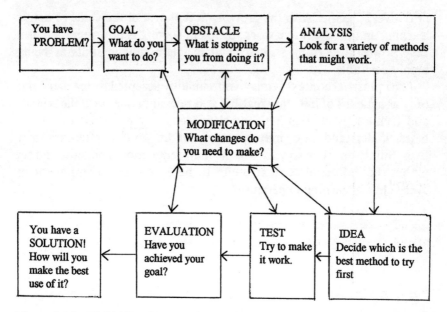

Figure 4.10   PAST 16 problem-solving model

- *Unit 1. What do we want to achieve?* – Stresses the importance of problem identification
- *Unit 2. Communicating effectively* – Focuses on the process of decision making.
- *Unit 3. Recognising constraints* – Appreciating that problem solving in industry requires working within the constraints of time, people, plant and materials.
- *Units 4 and 5* – involve the students in 'real world' problem solving experiences working alongside industrialists as process consultants.
- Finally students are offered a range of process questions to help them think more clearly about their purpose; what they want to achieve; their criteria for sucesss; the most appropriate action plan and the process of review.

Conclusions

Throughout the last decade there has been a fairly intensive growth of education–industry activity which has resulted in a significant number of exciting initiatives and classroom resources. As a result of some key initiatives, together with the growing acceptance of the value of active learning and investigative work, problem solving is now regarded as a very powerful learning strategy and problem solving skills as being highly desirable.

The industrial context is much more readily accepted by teachers, not only as a means of injecting real-life and relevant issues into the science and technology curriculum, but also because pupils need to have a better understanding of industry, the economy and its effect on their lives. Surely problem solving with its many educational benefits and set within the industrial context ought to be a necessary component of every child's learning experience?

CHAPTER FIVE

Environmental problem solving

Di Bentley, Roehampton Institute

This is my dream, that all the World is one –
Stones, trees, birds, men, light, Jesus and the Devil.
Fret not on any rung of change's spiral
For all is change and yet is one for ever:
Love, hate,crime, virtue fitting into one whole.
>   Turner (1984)

Other chapters in this book explore the nature of problem solving in detail. So what is it that makes **environmental** problem solving different? After all, is not the environment simply a context within which the problems are set, and in that respect no different to – say – chemistry or physics?

My response to that would be 'no'. For two reasons. First, because of the nature of environmental science itself and, second, the appeal of the environment as a global and complex – but real – context for young people (and in particular for girls) in which to study science. No other aspects of science brings together so thoroughly values, attitudes, complex variables and fundamental moral questions about the nature of science than do those which centre on the environment. In this chapter I look at environmental education in the UK as an area of study, particularly its reference points within the National Curriculum, and examine it as an example of 'holistic education'. I treat problem solving as an area of 'skills teaching' and cognitive development and then move from these realms of theory to more pragmatic issues by relating a case study of environmental problem solving amongst 13-year-old girls. I use that as the basis for advice and suggestions in planning environmental problem solving in classrooms, both primary and secondary.

Teaching about the environment – where are we?

Environmental issues have long been seen as an area of experience about which young people should learn. In the 1970s and early 1980s, for example, a large number of courses in CSE and O-level featured the word environment in their title. There were environmental science, environmental studies and environmental geography courses in which qualifications could be gained at 16. So, as a context for subject teaching, or as a cross-subject issue (at least in secondary education) environmental issues were seen as a legitimate area of study. Indeed, in their day, some of these courses were seen as being particularly innovative.

Primary schools also had themes or topics which featured the environment as an area of understanding so that in local and (as children became older) in global terms children became knowledge-able about the particular issues facing their communities.

With the coming of GCSE and, more importantly, the National Curriculum, the picture changed somewhat. The degree of flexibility has been reduced in many respects. Environmental issues are still a significant part of the curriculum in science, geography and history through the former National Curriculum's 'profile components' of knowledge and understanding, and appear in technology as a possible context for 'exploring a need'. There are, too, the National Curriculum's cross-curricular themes – of which environmental educa-tion is one. Much of the guidance produced by the National Curriculum Council in this cross-curricular area is valid, useful and important for future citizens to know and understand if they are to make important decisions about their communities, and the planet in general.

This is happening in schools at a time when environmental aware-ness in the general population is increasing. Newspaper articles, television programmes and books are published and refer to the consequences of environmental actions. Never before, then, have young people needed more knowledge to help understand envir-onmental alternatives and sort out fact from bias and from opinion. Young people themselves are expressing concerns and an interest both within school and outside on issues connected with the environment (Bentley, 1991). Yet in schools, the profile of environmental education is not as high as it was a decade ago as an area of study. All this is despite advice from the National Curriculum Council (NCC, 1990). The NCC's Curriculum Guide Number 7 contains a variety of ideas and suggestions for teaching environmental education as a cross-curricular theme. In the main their hypothesis is that there are three major purposes in teaching environmental education. These are to teach young people:

- *About the environment* – The scientific and technological knowledge and understanding that they will need in order to make informed decisions with regard to our planet.
- *In the environment*, so that they have the opportunity to observe the interactions and balances between different variables at first hand and appreciate the cyclic and dependent nature of living, physical and chemical processes.
- *For the environment*, so that they have the opportunity to explore the ideas, understandings and attitudes that will help them to be informed and concerned citizens into the next century.

(Adapted from NCC Curriculum Guide 7, p.7).

In the present state of flux with curriculum issues and curriculum control (and often where the expertise for the subject is not available in schools), the spirit of the National Curriculum's cross-curricular themes is not foremost in people's thinking – even with the best will in the world. Thus environmental issues are commonly taught within the knowledge and understanding of specific topics, but the cross-curricular themes are often put to one side in the sheer rush to fit everything in and assess it all. The flexibility to organise new courses and teach innovative areas has now effectively been lost to schools within the tight requirements of the curriculum. Resources for environmental education are lacking, too. In most schools, because environmental science is a cross-curricular area, resources come for the most part through the work of separate subject departments and are therefore fragmented and uncoordinated.

Problem solving in the environment

The NCC point out that one of the important contexts for teaching skills to pupils is that of problem solving. There are two essential issues to be considered in terms of environmental problem solving. One is that of problem solving itself, the other is the way in which this approach fits with the work that teachers must teach to children.

In the National Curriculum, the nature of problem solving fits best with Attainment Target 1 in science and with the 'design process' in technology. Figures 5.1 and 5.2 show how both environmental issues and problem solving skills can be fitted into the work of the National Curriculum in science and technology (adapted from Bentley, 1992 a, b; Fact sheets 5 and 6).

As I mentioned above, environmental issues also feature in particular areas of other content areas. As the NCC stipulates, we cannot afford to ignore these other subjects in the National Curriculum:

> Study of history, geography and religious education has a particularly important part to play in helping pupils clarify their values towards the environment.
> (*NCC Curriculum Guidance* 7, p.11)

The process of 'values clarification' is one to which I shall return in my closing argument. Figure 5.3 demonstrates how history and geography have much to offer in terms of working through issues of the environment (adapted from Bentley, 1992c; Fact sheet 7).

Cases in practice

The evidence from national projects like the CREST Awards Scheme (West, and Chandaman, 1993) bears out young people's interest in environment issues. In 1991, 20% of the projects submitted featured environmental aspects. There were some delightful projects: the detection of energy wastage in a large supermarket within 24 hours of its occurrence (instead of the normal 6 weeks at present); the management of the environment of dunes and urban areas. For example, a notable project developed publicity materials to raise awareness about conservation, including a video package made by the students themselves. Noisy environments featured in work with industry too, when students investigated strategies to reduce noise levels in a factory. This small selection indicates the enthusiasm of young people at a variety of ages. With this degree of enthusiasm, getting started is not a problem.

Watts (1992) and the CREST Award Scheme (1994) have some good ideas for starter projects such as:

- Conduct an energy survey of the school – how can electricity and fuel be saved?
- The school garden – are there ways to protect the environment, keep pests at bay?
- Is there a wild life area, a path of uncultivated land? What can be done to protect it?

- Is there a school pond or water nearby? Is it polluted?
- How clean is local air?
- Conduct a chemistry trail for pollution (see Burrows, 1984).
- What are CFCs – how can we monitor their use? How can we monitor the amount of lead on the roads around our school?
- Are the roads around the school safe? Do we need to slow traffic down? What is sound pollution? Is noise a sign of inefficient use of energy?

No doubt such problems pose management and resource problems for teachers. However, along with the difficulties there are also important benefits for teachers. To illustrate this, I describe a case study for which I am indebted to Tim Sibthorpe, director of the Wirral Science and Technology Regional Organisation (SATRO).

Case 1: A Structure for Primary/Secondary Environmental problem solving

This case illustrates a particular problem focus between a secondary school and its feeder primary schools. The science and technology teachers of the cluster of schools came together to discuss liaison in terms of the transfer from the primary schools at age 11. A decision was made to focus on the processes of science and technology rather than concerning themselves with the content of what pupils were taught. The group chose to develop a 3-year plan for primary environmental work; and the plan was organised so that pupils worked on local issues in the first year of the plan, on national issues in year two and on global issues in the third year. Teachers from both phases approached the work from a problem-solving viewpoint, leading to work in the secondary sector on CREST awards for the secondary pupils. In the first year of the plan, pupils tended to concentrate particularly on issues concerned with their playgrounds. This generated an enthusiasm for problem solving which furthered pupils' abilities in the processes in science and technology. In particular, the geography and science teachers in the secondary school were very supportive of the ways in which problem solving assisted an understanding of process issues. It gave the children opportunities to build, from a position of knowledge on these skills they had developed when arriving at secondary school.

All the problem-solving and environmental work was developed by primary schools in this example. When the pupils reached the secondary school, they had the opportunity to continue their work

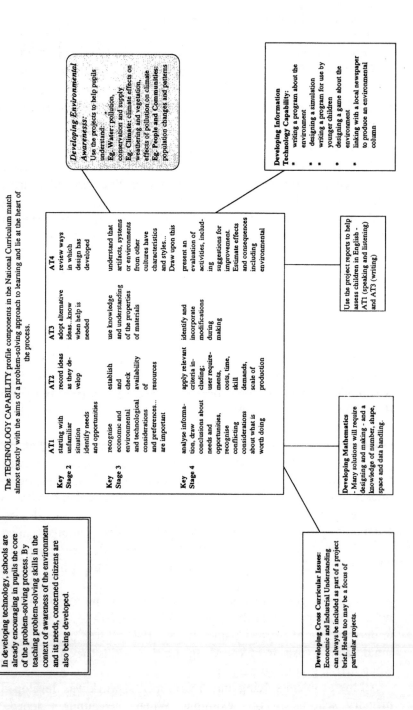

The TECHNOLOGY CAPABILITY profile components in the National Curriculum match almost exactly with the aims of a problem-solving approach to learning and lie at the heart of the process.

Developing Environmental Awareness:
Use the projects to help pupils understand:
Eg. Water: pollution, conservation and supply
Eg. Climate: climate effects on weathering and vegetation, effects of pollution on climate
Eg. People and Communities: population changes and patterns

Developing Information Technology Capability:
* writing a program about the environment
* designing a simulation
* writing a program for use by younger children
* designing a game about the environment
* linking with a local newspaper to produce an environmental column

In developing technology, schools are already encouraging in pupils the core of the problem-solving process. By teaching problem-solving skills in the context of awareness of the environment and its needs, concerned citizens are also being developed.

	AT1	AT2	AT3	AT4
Key Stage 2	starting with unfamiliar situation identify needs and opportunities	record ideas as they develop	adopt alternative ideas...know when help is needed	review ways in which design has developed
Key Stage 3	recognise economic and environmental and technological considerations and preferences... are important	establish and check availability of resources	use knowledge and understanding of the properties of materials	understand that artifacts, systems or environments from other cultures have characteristics and styles... Draw upon this
Key Stage 4	analyse information, draw conclusions about needs and opportunities, recognise conflicting considerations about what is worth doing	apply relevant criteria including; user requirements, costs, time, skill demands, scale of production	identify and incorporate modifications during making	present an evaluation of activities, including suggestions for improvement. Estimate effects and consequences including environmental

Use the project reports to help assess children in English - AT1 (speaking and listening) and AT3 (writing)

Developing Mathematics - Many solutions will require designing and making - and a knowledge of number, shape, space and data handling.

Developing Cross Curricular Issues: Economic and Industrial Understanding can always be included as part of a project brief. Health too may be a focus of particular projects.

Figure 5.1

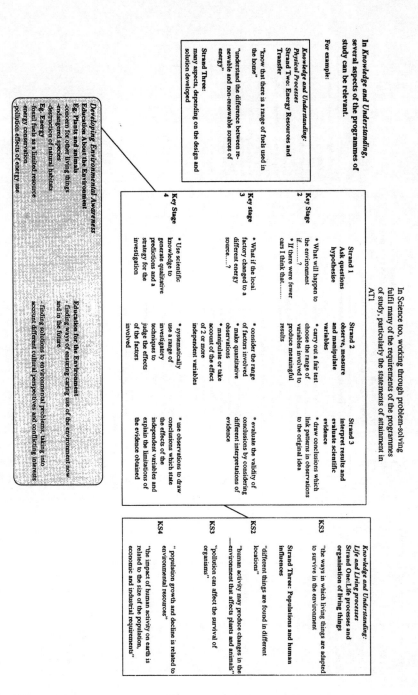

Figure 5.2

86

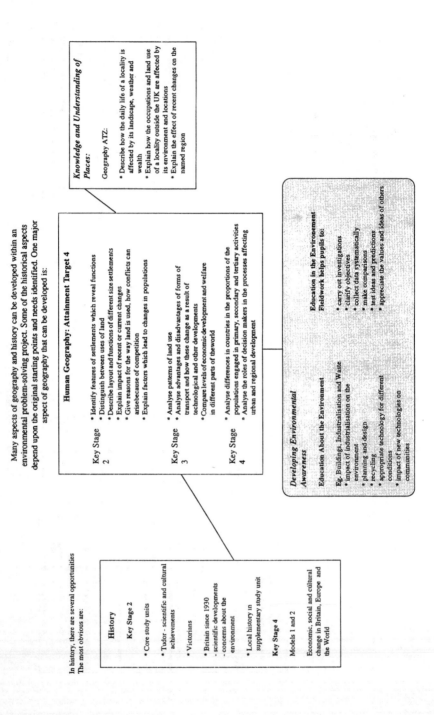

Many aspects of geography and history can be developed within an environmental problem-solving project. Some of the historical aspects depend upon the original starting points and needs identified. One major aspect of geography that can be developed is:

Human Geography: Attainment Target 4

Key Stage 2
* Identify features of settlements which reveal functions
* Distinguish between uses of land
* Describe layout and functions of different size settlements
* Explain impact of recent or current changes
* Give reasons for the way land is used, how conflicts can arise because of competition
* Explain factors which lead to changes in populations

Key Stage 3
* Analyse patterns of land use
* Analyse advantages and disadvantages of forms of transport and how these change as a result of technological and other developments
* Compare levels of economic development and welfare in different parts of the world

Key Stage 4
* Analyse differences in countries in the proportions of the populations engaged in primary, secondary and tertiary activities
* Analyse the roles of decision makers in the processes affecting urban and regional development

Knowledge and Understanding of Places:

Geography ATZ:

* Describe how the daily life of a locality is affected by its landscape, weather and wealth
* Explain how the occupations and land use of a locality outside the UK are affected by its environment and locations
* Explain the effect of recent changes on the named region

Developing Environmental Awareness

Education About the Environment

Eg. Buildings, Industrialisation and Waste
* impact of industrialisation on the environment
* planning and design
* recycling
* appropriate technology for different conditions
* impact of new technologies on communities

Education in the Environment
Fieldwork helps pupils to:
* carry out investigations
* clarify objectives
* collect data systematically
* make comparisons
* test ideas and predictions
* appreciate the values and ideas of others

In history, there are several opportunities. The most obvious are:

History

Key Stage 2
* Core study units
* Tudor - scientific and cultural achievements
* Victorians
* Britain since 1930
  - scientific developments
  - concerns about the environment
* Local history in supplementary study unit

Key Stage 4
Models 1 and 2
Economic, social and cultural change in Britain, Europe and the World

Figure 5.3

during the first 3 months, at the end of which the teachers from the primary school came to an award-giving day to hand out the certificates to successful ex-pupils, thereby maintaining the links and ensuring continuity of intention and practice.

Ideologies of education and learning

From an example of good practice I want to move on to the development of better practice. In this sense, I think it is important to place approaches to learning such as problem solving within a broader ideological framework for education. Environmental education, with its implications for social re-examination and value clarification, needs to be contextualised. This is particularly important with regard to the later arguments that I shall present in regard to the peculiar relevance of both problem solving and environmental issues to education for young women.

Skilbeck (1976) has suggested that there at least three basic education ideologies: classical humanism, progressivism and reconstructionism.

Lawton (1983) describes classical humanism as being essentially knowledge-centred, progressivism as being child-centred, and reconstructionism as being society-centred. Indeed Skilbeck himself describes reconstructionist ideology as having the characteristics of: 'a conception of learning and the acquisition of knowledge as an active social process involving projects and problem solving strategies guided, but not dominated by teachers'.

In the work of the Secondary Science Curriculum Review (1985) which over the decade of its development was to have a profound effect upon science education in general and the direction of the National Curriculum in particular, a fourth ideological stance was described. It is this stance of 'holism' which finds its home most comfortably within problem solving and environmental education:

'What we mean by holism is an ideology in which the self-esteem of the learner, the development of conceptual understanding from the starting point of the leaner's personally held ideas . . . and the development of self empowerment are seen as being key principles . . . . Whilst it provides youngsters with the facility to participate fully in the decision making processes of democracy, it also takes into account their personal attributes, understandings and personal developments. It implies a learning environment in which responsibility for self and others becomes all important

whereby the youngsters are encouraged to become active participants in the learning process.'
(Bentley, Ellington and Stewart, 1985 p.663).

As an ideology, holism brings together both the individual and her or his values and ideas, along with active learning (such as one might experience in problem solving) and responsibility for others (as a concerned citizen). Indeed Bentley *et al.* go on to say that:

'holism places value on the life experiences of youngsters in the context of their development of scientific rationality . . . it also views this development as being one that is enhanced by their personal self-empowerment to make decisions and solve problems in a social political and economic framework.'
(Bentley, Ellington and Stewart, 1985 p.663).

Holism, then, is an important ideological concept that draws together both environmental education and problem-solving approaches to learnii g. But why should holistic education be important? I would argue that it is an approach to education and in particular to thinking that is important for all pupils to understand, but is one that appeals to girls and women very specifically. In a recent piece of research by Birke (1992) into the views of women on a science course in adult education run for women only , the women (of ages 25 to 50) mentioned topics that they thought might be relevant to a course for women. As Birke states:

'[these] reflected women's domestic role – wanting to know more about science in the home . . . and a concern for our global future.

'In recording topics they would like to cover:
topical environmental issues were also noted, such as garden pesticides and global warming.'

Case 2: Sandra

Not only older women have these views about the environment and the need for ownership of science. A case study of the views of Sandra, a 13-year-old young women making choices for her science education future, in Bentley (1985) reveals similar ideas. Sandra's experiences of science education supports those of a rule-bound process which is the embodiment of 'right answers', a view in sympathy with the findings of Carre (1981). It comes as no surprise that her view of science is an empiricist–inductivist as described by Cawthorne and Rowell (1978) and Zylbersztajn (1983) in terms of how science teachers traditionally portray science. For example Sandra says:

> S. Well, take physics. We did some experiments on Ohm's law, and laws of gravity and things like that. You know its all laws. You can't find out new things about laws can you? When they've been discovered by famous men, they're not going to be wrong are they? Laws are a bit unchangeable aren't they?
> I. Perhaps . . . .
> S. Well its not like parliament is it? Where you can change the laws if you don't like them. These are the laws of nature aren't they?

Sandra also advocates a much more autonomous and holistic approach to science education. She demands the opportunity to be trusted to work things out for herself, and quite plainly sees the failure of her science teachers to allow her this opportunity as an issue of responsibility and control.

> S. I think I would have liked to live in the days when we didn't know so much about science.
> I. Why?
> S. So I could find out for myself. You know like Newton. I thought when I heard that story, I could have worked out that things fell and so something must be pulling them. But nowadays they've found out all the easy things. You need computers and lots of complicated apparatus to find out new things now. I'd like to really discover something new. Not world shattering, just new, that no one else knew.

She makes a powerful plea for a science that belongs to her:

> S. I think we should have just one lesson a week when we can do our kind of science.
> I. Your kind of science?
> S. Yes I want time to find out about my ideas in science.
> I. Is that what you meant when you said in your questionnaire 'less theory . . . more enterprise'?
> S. Yes, I'd like it to be my choice. You know, like this nuclear stuff .
> I. Nuclear stuff?
> S. Yes, like we use it to make electricity but it's dangerous and it affects health and stuff. Does it really, why do we do it if it's dangerous? Can't we find a better way, before the earth gets damaged? Why aren't we being careful?
> I. Is that science?

S. Well, it's about physics isn't it? and it's about measuring things and comparing them. We do that in science.

I. So science is about measuring and comparing?

S. Well not just about that.

I. What else?

S. Well . . . looking at things . . . observing, and getting results after an experiment. I suppose its about experiments really.

I. And nuclear things?

S. Yes . . . well . . . how they affect us and our bodies and the earth . . . and our children.

I. I see. So you'd really like to do more for yourself in science?

S. Yes, prove something for myself . . . you know, my own theories . . . .

I. Such as?

S. Well . . . its difficult isn't it? But I do have ideas about things sometimes . . . you know, you wonder why something happens and sometimes you'd like to find out more.

I. Wouldn't that make life difficult for teachers? If everyone was doing a different experiment?

S. It would be difficult, yes. But if we could do it maybe they'd trust us more . . . you know, let us get stuff for ourselves, and plan our own bits. They really treat us like kids. We're not encouraged to be . . . well . . . enterprising.

I. Why do you think that is?

S. It's like you said . . . what if we all wanted to do different things . . . they couldn't cope, or control us. They don't think we can organise ourselves enough.

The change of the image and practice of science as it occurs in science education is a plea being echoed by the clients. As Griffiths (1976) suggests, women:

> don't want to participate more fully in a science which is patriarchal, hierarchical and authoritarian, and which is used to oppress and exploit the mass of people in the interests of the few.

Feminine Science and technology

Sandra, like the women in Birke's study, is supporting Manthorpe's (1982) four major areas of 'feminine science':

- A holistic view in which social, ethical and moral questions are unquestionably involved.

- A scientific community based on co-operation.
- Respect for and equal valuations of different forms of knowledge
  – including the irrational and the subjective.
- Placing emphasis on a re-uniting of the intellect and emotion and
  a revaluation . . . of the belief that the quality of life has priority
  over economics.

(Manthorpe, 1982)

So holism for young women involves both the approach and the subject matter. In my view this makes environmental problem solving an ideal vehicle for enabling students to view science in particular as part of a holistic framework of the world in which we live.

Case 3: Pensby School

This case study deals with a week-long problem-solving event for Year 9 girls at a secondary school, designed to focus and harness their enthusiasm and energy. I am grateful to Tim Sibthorpe for this case, too. Several months before the event, a team of teachers, SATRO (Science And Technology Regional Organisation) leaders, and industrialists, came together to plan the week. On each occasion across the 3 years in which the event has been running there has been a different context for the problems. In the description below, the context was that of energy. The planning team organised the context, problem selection day, a field trip and team support.

Contextualising day

This day involved key-note speakers setting the scene for the girls. Wherever possible, women industrialists were chosen to act as role-models as well as 'scene setters' and were also part of the planning team. After their input, problem-solving issues were discussed and the girls were reminded of the two basic principles for the problem-solving week – those of sustainability and appropriateness. These two principles were to be addressed as criteria to any problem which the girls chose to investigate during the week. The role of the team approach in problem solving was discussed and pupils were asked to split up into teams to focus on the problems they wished to address. They were given a task to help them frame their problem. They were asked to prepare two lists. The first was a list of 'energy words and contexts' such as coal, wind and gas; and the second list was called 'implications'. Here the girls listed issues such as insulation, cost and renewability. They were then asked to link any words they liked in list 1 in some way to list 2. So they might, for example link coal to cost or renewability, which could lead to the investigation of alternative energy sources, since coal is a non-renewable resource. In this way they were helped to frame their problem and, by the end of the day, they were expected to have produced a coherent statement of their investigative problem-solving work, supported by teachers.

The projects

Such focused activity gave rise to a variety of problems. The girls spent the rest of the week investigating these and other tasks of their own choosing, supported by staff across a range of subjects to assist them in design, scientific problem solving, realisation of design and reporting. Two are of special note. In one project, the girls linked light to energy. They began with an audit of lighting in the school, and this then mushroomed into the effects of lighting conditions on staff and work environments. It involved the health and safety officer for the school, and members of the council health and safety executive. They looked at the choice of light bulbs the school made in terms of cost, longevity and consumption, assisted by staff, industrialists and governors and explored the health issues of lighting levels for work in different parts of the school, conducting surveys, administering questionnaires and drawing scale maps.

In the second project, the focus was a look at river pollution. The school is close to the confluence of the rivers Dee and Mersey and the girls wished to work on an automatic water sampler that would provide information about the level of pollution of the rivers. During the week they designed and made a remote monitor, which took the form of a buoy with sensors attached to sample the water content and relay this information back to a computer. During the process of the development the girls used a large number of complex scientific ideas and adapted them to their needs in terms of electronics, corrosion, remote monitoring, etc.

This case study highlights several issues, but the most important are those of ownership of the problems by the pupils. They organised to ensure that the activities were smooth running, that there was co-operation between several groups such as teachers, industrialists and other outsiders from schools taking place, and that students knew and understood the objectives of the exercise.

Conclusion

What is needed is something that can appeal to young people, and give them the opportunity to put the knowledge and skills they are acquiring in school to good use – something that picks up on the interest and enthusiasm and concern that young people are demonstrating already at a variety of ages. I believe that problem solving is the answer to that 'something' because it allows ownership and creative imagination to be developed. The issues of the environment are precisely those that will engage the enthusiasm and interest of students in a way which encourages participation in full. Girls in particular find the complexity of the variables and the holism of the approach very satisfying.

SECTION THREE

Extending learners

This section discusses the extension of problem solving across a variety of learners – with great variations in need

CHAPTER SIX

GETSET and go: problem solving for girls

Mike Watts, Roehampton Institute and Alan West, CREST Award Scheme

There is some well-documented evidence to suggest that the contexts of science and technology are vital to the successful completion of problem-solving tasks. One indication of this is given by Murphy (1988) when she says:

> 'The same problem was set to 13–year-olds in two contexts, everyday and scientific . . . . More than 50 per cent of pupils carried out an effective quantitative approach in the science setting compared with 25 per cent for the everyday investigation. The context dominates the actual problem presented and dictates the solution.'

We describe here an experiment in 'feminising' (Watts and Bentley, 1994) problem solving by adopting two main features:

1. A specific event for girls only, so that they were 'in their element' and without the competitive distraction of having boys in the way.
2. Shaping the context of problem solving to have 'human appeal'. This is a point developed in other chapters.

The GETSET event

The event was organised by the CREST Awards Scheme and called 'GETSET' (Girls Entering Tomorrow's Science Engineering and Technology) and was spurred by the national levels of participation of girls in the CREST scheme. Figure 6.1 shows the peak numbers for participation to be at bronze level, age 14.

While this is a very encouraging figure, there is then a rapid fall-off

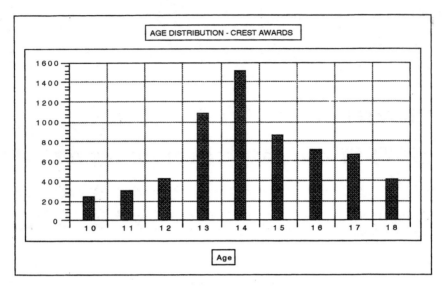

Figure 6.1 Indicative national participation by girls at Bronze Award level

as girls become eligible the next stages of the scheme. The aim was to stimulate the appetite of many more girls for problem solving at CREST Silver and Gold Award levels (Figure 6.2). The GETSET event was organised for some 400 girls at key stage 3 (14 years old), over a 2-day period, with accommodation provided for the intervening night. It took place through the generosity of sponsors and a large holiday camp in the seaside town of Skegness. A range of adults and assistants were on hand to help, the primary groups being the teachers accompanying the girls to the event and a team of mentors. These were women scientist and engineer volunteers from commerce and industry who participated for the 2 days to help and support the problem solving, and to act as role models for the girls as they worked.

Creating human contexts

As has been noted elsewhere (West and Chandaman, 1993), extended problem solving which is real and relevant is too frequently squeezed out of course time under examination requirements, and yet it is very often experience of this kind that can prove to be an important indicator to those involved in recruiting into courses and into industry. It is quite common that a premium is placed on core skills which embrace problem solving, communication and teamwork, and yet these do not form part of assessment in schools.

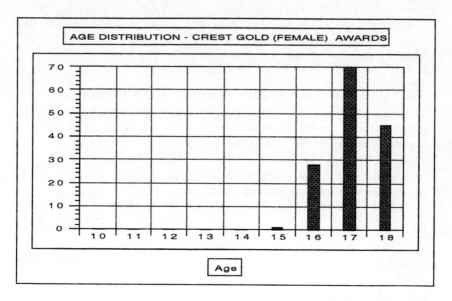

Figure 6.2   Indicative numbers of girls entering for Gold Awards

The context for the problems for the GETSET event was provided by a 'survival challenge' as follows:

The rogue asteroid 'Oopsorry' has passed very close to the earth, causing Tidal Waves, Earthquakes, Tornadoes and weather slightly worse than normal. As a result there has been a complete breakdown in services (Gas, Electricity, Water), and other than yourselves, there is no help at hand. The question now is 'Can you survive until help arrives, or things get back to normal?'

Luckily you find yourself inside the 'Funcoast Holiday Camp' with a large fence around it. Law and order outside the camp has completely broken down, but the marauding bands of looters are not aware of anything of value in the camp, so you are safe from them, so far.

However, your main concern is the safety of 24 (hypothetical) under-5's stranded with you. They are frightened and cold. They have two nurses with them but THEY NEED YOUR HELP.

In four sessions you will tackle four groups of projects:

SURVIVAL
ENGINEERING
WATER MANAGEMENT
SITE MANAGEMENT

There were then a series of problems within each of these main areas so that, for example, the *survival* problems appeared as:

You are isolated within the camp until the emergency situation returns to normal, or help arrives. You need to ensure the survival of the 24 young children, their two nurses and yourselves.

(a) Rationing

You have found a list of available stores that are not contaminated. You must draw up a basic rationing system to feed the children (One Diet) and yourselves and 2 nurses (Separate Diet). This is important, so get it done quickly, the children are already hungry.

You will be judged on:

- The diet's nutritional components.
- The diet's variety and accurate quantities.
- Your guesstimates of the nutritional value of the diet.

(b) Body Warming

You must keep yourselves and the children warm. From available materials, design and make a Body Warmer that is efficient and comfortable.

You will be judged on:

- The design and durability of the garment
- Its success in tests for heat retention/comfort
- Appearance, as YOU model your garment against 12 others.

(c) Inner Warmth

Hot food is essential, so you must devise a Soup Heating Process, using the chemicals provided. You will have a British Forces Hot Can to study, now design your own.

You will be judged on:

- The maximum heat achieved under test conditions.

Each girl was in a team of eight, each team was assigned a mentor who was only to help with a resource problem within the project (e.g. some equipment that was missing or unusable) but not to assist in any way with solutions. In each room was a Master Judge and three pairs of judges to allocate marks and the teams were provided with criteria for the judging of each problem. Teams were organised to ensure a mix of schools and friends, and the winning teams were awarded prizes. The criteria for judgement were detailed in this way for the *engineering* section:

Bridging a gap:
- Design of your Bridge:
  - *Has a design been produced on paper?*
  - *Has any form of calculation been attempted?*
  - *Have appropriate materials been chosen for the design?*
- Its efficiency in carrying loads
  - *Will the structure support itself across the chasm?*

- *Can it be built and erected from one side?*
- *How many people will it carry?*
● Extra marks will be given if it will hold 2 or 3 people at one time. Proceed to bonus test only if structure appears capable of withstanding load.

Harness the Wind:
● Efficiency, sturdiness
  - *Has a design been produced on paper?*
  - *Has any form of calculation been attempted?*
  - *Have appropriate materials been chosen for the design?*
● Design ingenuity
  - *Does the design work as a structure?*
  - *Will the windmill raise a load? What load?*
  - *Innovative design bonus?*

Water Purification:
● The quality (at least 4 bottles full)
  - *Quality of design and testing of system – does it work? Will it clog?*
● Clarity
  - *Measured clarity using a colorimeter*
● Technology, equipment and methods

The girls were required to get to know each other and work as a team, and there were a range of social and 'funtime' events in the intervening evening to make the overall two days interesting and fun. The tasks were varied, demanding and required a range of scientific, technological, creative, communicative and social skills.

The context for the problem solving activities were related to the venue in which the girls found themselves, i.e. a ring-fenced holiday camp. It was not a laboratory or a technology workshop, and in this sense all of the activities relied on the girls using appropriate technology and readily available materials. In this case they needed to be using their skills and ingenuity, together with the available materials, to meet a challenging need. The theme for the problem challenges needed to be strong, cohesive (in that they are all working for a common purpose and being constructed in such a way that there are regular opportunities for review, praise and sharing of experience). The 'Oopssorry' Survival Challenge presented an appropriate context: it was the *survival* aspect, with its linked *caring issues*, that were brought to the fore, rather than the negative aspects of such a disaster.

Evaluation

While there were the inevitable hiccoughs in organising a programme for so many diverse individuals and groups, the event was a marked success and part of the ensuing evaluation brought forward the following comments, first from mentors:

'Good ideas. Planning and teamwork are an essential part of engineering and enable better decisions, sharing of ideas etc. and these should be emphasised.'

'Projects were good – sufficient detail to know what was required, but not so much as to give the game away.'

'I really enjoyed myself – I learnt from the kids!'

'A most enjoyable two days, I left very encouraged by the creativity of many of the children and by their enthusiastic approach.'

'I believe that the course was successful in opening up the image of Science and Technology to girls. The girls were of the appropriate age for this type of programme. It was very satisfying and I was immensely pleased to see such a large attendance of girls.'

The teachers gave comments such as:

'The theme of the activity was a nice idea and generally the girls enjoyed themselves. The only real criticism I can voice is that the activities overran their time.'

'Excellent – the right balance of aspects of science and technology.'

'Overall the girls had an informative, stimulating and worthwhile experience. One of them commented that it was the first time she had had to think for herself!'

'I found it extremely valuable in being able to talk to mentors about what lured them into Science and Technology. I would like to congratulate the team of organisers of a really brilliant event. There were difficulties but, with such a fast-moving programme, they did not detract from the enjoyment and achievement of the pupils.'

'GETSET has achieved its purpose in our school. Our group was mostly a selection of those with exceptional ability and interest in Science. They have talked of little else since they came back to school and the rest of the year group is green with envy. The activities brought out the real problem solving excitement of Science and Techology which is sadly being relegated to the "back burner" by schools.'

Comments from the girls were elicited, too, during the two days and these were almost exclusively enthusiastic and tinged with excitement (Bentley, 1993). In general terms, they too saw the contexts as appropriate and satisfying, and the event presented opportunities for many of them to take some responsibility for their own results and conclusions.

It is too early to say whether the original aim of GETSET has been achieved: to encourage more girls into the later stages of CREST – and eventually, into careers in science and technology. There are plans for further events and the follow-up is just beginning.

CHAPTER SEVEN

Project treasure hunt: the quest for science in special schools

Tony Hamaker, London Borough of Greenwich

This chapter describes a project trialled in two special schools to investigate the possibility of developing a problem-solving methodology in science lessons with students who have special educational needs.

It suggests that such an approach is possible and highlights the advantages of the methdology in helping to raise the expectation and self esteem of such students.

School A is a school for students with emotional and behavioural difficulties. School B is a school for students with severe physical disabilities. The number of students participating was seven from school A and nine from school B.

The background

In schools for children with emotional and behavioural difficulties, the problems associated with the move towards more flexible learning approaches may pose a threat to pupils' personal confidence and self esteem, creating feelings of anxiety, insecurity and fear of personal failure.

In addition, there may be a lack of experience and associated confidence in practical investigatory science for teachers working with students in EBD schools. Indeed a similar situation may well exist for teachers working with students with severe physical disabilities, although the problems that such students may have will be somewhat different to those encountered in an EBD school.

'Project Treasure Hunt' attempts to develop a problem solving approach to science, utilising as far as is possible the Programmes of

Study and Attainment Targets outlined under Sc 1 of the National Curriculum:

1. Adopting principles and an approach outlined in the CASE project (Adey, Shayer and Yates, 1990) in that it attempts to encourage the development of thinking and reasoning from concrete to formal operational. In so doing it makes use of some of the types of reasoning patterns which are characteristic of formal operations (Adey, Shayer and Yates, 1989):
   - control and variables and exclusion of irrelevant variables;
   - compensation and equilibrium;
   - combinations;
   - ratio and proportionality;
   - classification.

2. Adopting a problem-solving methodology, in that, as Watts (1991) describes, 'the pivotal virtue of problem solving is as a means of transferring some of the responsibility and ownership for learning to the learner.'

The initial need for 'Project Treasure Hunt' came from the two schools themselves. It was agreed that the main aims of this project was to show that:

- students are capable of organising their own learning needs;
- science is a fun activity;
- the processes are accessible to all;
- problem solving in science and technology is an activity associated with all cultures;
- problem-solving activities in science and technology can be developed by teachers with a limited experience in those domains (provided adequate support is initially available).

The design of the product

Treasure Hunt involves students trying to find the location of hidden treasure by completing a number of problem solving activities, leading to coded clues, which may or may not identify the exact location of the prize. Students have to determine the precise position or location of the treasure.

The teacher is responsible for hiding the treasure by devising a statement which gives its exact location. This statement can then be split up into simpler 'bits of information'. The actual statement and the number of 'bits of information' will depend on what the teacher believes is realistic for the class to attempt and complete.

Each 'bit of information' is coded, but can be discovered by the completion of each of the problem-solving activities. The code has to be broken before the information becomes clear. Students are never told the code or how to break it but clues are given within each activity. As the code is slightly different for each activity, the student will have to use the same processes to break each code. An example of such a statement could be as follows:

THE TREASURE IS:
BEHIND THE FIRST AID POSTER/WHICH IS ABOVE THE SINK/
IN THE SCIENCE ROOM/LABORATORY 4/ON THE GROUND
FLOOR/OF THE LIBRARY BLOCK.

In this example the code is based on a simple number system corresponding to the letters of the alphabet. Thus, A = 1, B = 2, C = 3 . . . Y = 25, Z = 26. For each subsequent activity in question the code is slightly displaced. Thus A = 26 when Z = 25, etc.

Consider the following part of a statement which includes three misleading 'bits of information'.

The correct 'bit of information is (A) ON THE GROUND FLOOR. Three other 'wrong' bits of information could include the following;

(B) ON THE TOP FLOOR; (C) ON THE BASEMENT FLOOR; (D) OUTSIDE THIS BUILDING.

The codes for these statements assuming A = 1, B = 2 . . . etc., are:

(A) 1514/2085/7181521144/6121515181.
(B) 1514/2085/201516/612151518.
(C) 1514/2085/211951351420/612151518.
(D) 15212019945/208919/22191249147.

The students are not told at the end of each activity whether they have a correct solution or not. They have to complete all activities and discover a completed location. If this location does not correspond to that devised by the teacher, the students are told of this and are asked to re-evaluate each activity in order to trace where a mistake could be. In this way they have to check over their work carefully in order to repeat measurements, observations etc., or to re-design their plans.

The problem-solving activities that were set can be described as either GIVEN or GOAl problems

- *Given* – where the solver is given both the goal and possible strategies (by specifying the equipment to use).

- *Goal* – where the solver has to decide and develop own strategies (Watts, 1991).

Furthermore, each problem solving activity is of a *closed* nature, having only one correct solution. This is important since it allows the teacher to assign a number of 'wrong' answers to each problem solving activity. If a degree of care and accuracy is missing from each activity then a 'wrong' answer is obtained which has its associated 'bit of information'. The decoded statement then does not correspond to the real location of the treasure.

At each problem-solving activity there is an associated work card headed STATION ONE . . . STATION THREE . . . etc. Next to this heading will be an associated number in brackets corresponding to the particular heading. By relating this number to the letters of the heading, the students will have the basis for cracking the code. As the code is slightly displaced for each activity, the student will have to use the same process to crack the code for each actvity.

In setting up this project, the teacher had to complete the following steps:

- Decide upon where the treasure was to be found ensuring that the overall statement could be split into a manageable number of 'bits of information'.
- Each 'bit of information' was allocated to a particular activity area.
- Each activity area had other wrong 'bits of information' allocated to it, the number of wrong bits being what the teacher regarded as manageable.
- Each 'bit of information' was then coded according to the code devised/allocated to each activity area.
- The problem-solving activities had to be designed and tested and then allocated to each of the designated activity areas with the associated correct answer.
- Wrong answers or a range of wrong answers were then allocated to each of the problem-solving activities.
- The equipment had to be produced and put into respective trays/ drawers for easy access.

The problem-solving activities included the following examples:

- Students were asked to construct a pendulum clock to give a certain number of swings in 1 minute. They were asked to find out the length and the mass needed to give this number of swings. They had to use strategies involving control of variables, equilibrium and compensation.

- Students were asked to calculate how much it would cost to send a parcel through the post and hence how much change they would get from £5. They had to design a way of weighing the parcel without the use of scales or a balance. They had to use strategies in control of variables, compensation, ratio and proportionality.
- Students were asked to discover the identities of five rocks, were given some chemicals and an information key to help them. They had to use a classification strategy.
- Students were asked to identify the names of four chemicals from patterns of information given to them about what happened when certain chemical combinations occurred. They had to design and carry out their investigation. They had to use strategies involving combinatorial reasoning, control of variables and classification.
- Students were given a number of chemicals and asked to determine which one was water. They were given information about water and how it reacted with certain chemicals. They had to use strategies involving combinatorial reasoning and control of variables.
- Students were given a number of bottles of pure chemicals along with mixtures of the pure chemicals and asked to find out which bottles contained the mixtures. They had to use strategies involving combinatorial reasoning, control of variables and classification.
- Students were given a numerical problem involving a lateral thinking strategy and a combinations strategy.

School A allocated 1 × 2 hour session for 4 weeks to complete its version of Treasure Hunt. School B allocated 2 × 2 hour sessions per werk for 4 weeks to complete its version of Treasure Hunt.

The equipment for each activity was shared between schools and consisted of whatever the schools could muster. The problem-solving activities were designed with this in mind. Both schools had support throughout from the TVEI science advisory teacher who acted as the link between the schools. Prepared sheets were used with each activity to help record measurements, observations, conclusions etc. Written and taped evaluations of the project were made by the students at the end of the 4-week period.

Students' evaluations

The following comments are transcriptions of the comments made by individuals at the end of their investigation stage. The students were asked to record their comments on to a cassette tape.

The teachers have also added further points to help clarify some of the student comments by putting them into some form of context where needed.

School A: student evaluation

STEPHEN

'I did 5 experiments. I found it half-and-half boring. The pendulum and counting was boring. I felt tired because all you did was look at the watch and count. Not exciting like using bunsen burners.

'Finding the clues was interesting but I wanted food to be the prize. I was disappointed with the pen. Breaking the code was interesting because of finding out where the treasure was.

'We should find out for ourselves. You should not give us sheets telling us what to do. We needed teachers to help us solve the problems. We asked them what to do, but they only helped us with reading.

'I liked it but the prize was boring. They, the teachers, showed us what to do like using the spoons and droppers to put things in cups.

'I wanted to work on my own. It was easy on my own. Micky shouted in my ear. "give me this, give me that". Micky took the sheet away to do the writing. He said that I couldn't write and was thick. Micky is a plonker, thinks he is the boss; thinks I am his slave or something. I would have preferred to work with Mark all of the time. Micky would not take it in turns.'

MARK

'It was boring. I had to keep repeating things. I had to show Tony the boring bits. I was interested in the experiment bit although I was mucking around at first, weighing the box. I liked using the acids the best. I liked that bit.'

LLOYD

'I liked the teasure hunt idea, the fun and games idea. Liked to think about the problems and working out the solutions. I didn't like the pendulum. I had trouble with the pendulum. I got it wrong but looked at the pattern of results to work out a right answer. I didn't think that I would need to do the experiment again but did and my pattern was now right.'

'I liked being on my own but would like to be in a group to share the work load. I wouldn't mind being told what to do but I liked the idea of investigating. I like practical work and want to do more. I liked the acid one, recording the results and making combinations. I liked the extension task. I enjoyed the thinking. I like thinking things through.'

School A: a teacher's additional comments

The first point that I would like to stress is that some of the comments have to be decoded. This is a result of pupils' limited ability to articulate ideas, or something to do with the nature of their personal/ learning difficulties or both. What may appear to be contradictory may in fact be quite consistent and positive from the pupil's point of view.

Stephen's comment about the pendulum 'being boring' more realistically relates to great personal difficulty in concentration, which this investigation tended to highlight. Stephen also has a tremendous need to be 'gratified' quickly in terms of an activity being completed or rewarded. The requirement of disciplined repetition and recording, as part of this investigation, delayed for an unsatisfactory length of time the reward of achieving a result from his point of view.

The comments he made in relation to his desire to have food as the prize (treasure) is a reflection of his tremendous need for nurture and gratification. Comments about things being boring probably also reflect his relatively low conceptual ability, as indicated by a Science Reasoning Task that was administered to him prior to the commencement of the project.

Mark is a similar case in these regards, with respect to his comments. Both Stephen and Mark are effectively non-readers. Hence negative comments about the investigation instruction sheets and their misconception that these sheets told them what to do. Teachers did not in fact 'tell them what to do' but rather emphasised the notion of problem solving for themselves or in their groups. Teachers were very careful not to tell pupils any strategies for solving the problems set. The pupil's perceptions of teachers telling them what to do is really a way of saying that pupils asked teachers lots of questions and that much teacher/pupil interaction took place. It is worth noting that the frequency of such interaction diminished as pupil confidence grew.

The actual nature of the teacher/pupil interaction was that of teachers asking pupils questions in response to questions. In this way pupils' own ideas were simply reflected back to them.

The one area that we did really give help was in the practical skill area of showing the pupils the best ways to use a spoon, measuring cylinder, etc.

Mark's reference to 'mucking around' indicates a phase that many of the pupils went through at some time. This was more like 'playing' or 'trial and error' rather than bad behaviour. This was an important stage to go through for them because through their play they actually began to discover ways of solving the problems posed. Once they began to discover strategies for investigating, their confidence grew and pupils felt that they could then do the investigations.

The notion of solving problems and finding clues which lead to a treasure location, consistently came across as a series of events which motivated pupils to do the investigations. The pupils were perhaps unaware of just how much they were learning and progressing by completing each investigation and this had to be fed back to them continuously in positive affirmation of success and the encouragement of praise in what they were doing.

Overall, pupils at the end of the project felt that they had achieved much and felt good about most of what they had done. For pupils, who feel bad about themselves for most of the time, this was a tremendous filip and perhaps more important and significant than the acutal experience and learning that occurred.

Certainly their confidence and staff confidence to engage in practical work has been boosted enormously and the demand now is for more and more next term.

School B: student evaluation

PAUL

'I enjoyed everything. I like doing experiments. I liked it because it was like the Crystal Maze. I found it difficult to use the equipment. I understood how to break the code, but needed help from Nicky to put it all down in writing. Working in a group was better than working on my own because I could give ideas.

'It could have been harder. It should have had harder clues. I learnt how I could cope with things not going to plan.'

SIMON

'I enjoyed doing experiments, things, not listening to lots of talking. I enjoyed telling someone how to do it. I thought all of the problems were hard. I felt that what was asked was difficult, too scientific. I learnt more about science and interesting experiments. I know now that I am very good.

'There should have been more computers in it.

'I think I'm very good at cooperating in groups. I learnt how problems are solved.'

NICKY

'I worked in a group while I did the science. I enjoyed all the work that we had to do. It was different to what we normally have to do and I think that was why I enjoyed it. I enjoyed the acid station and the rock station. I enjoyed breaking the codes after each station because it gave a clue to where the treasure was. I learnt how to solve new problems and break codes. I learnt how to solve problems within a group.

'The thing that I found most difficult was getting started. After reading the sheets that told us what to do, it was difficult because we had all these things sitting on a table in front of us and we didn't know what to do with it. I found breaking the code quite easy once I got started. I didn't find any of it really easy but once I got started it got easier.

'I think there are benefits of working in a group because you can support each other, like if someone can't use their hands to lift things then someone else in the group can do it for them. If someone doesn't know what to do then the other one that knows can say what to do. I gained knowledge. I learnt different ways of working things out. I got to know more of what other people knew. Everybody in the group was helping in some way, even if they couldn't write or something, they were still giving ideas and suggestions. We had to compromise quite a few times because one said one idea and the other said something else so the one who didn't have an idea could say that we tried one of the ideas first and then try the other idea.

'I don't think it could have been better because it was very enjoyable. I think that this type of science should go in all schools.'

DANIEL

'I enjoyed working out the clues and solving the problems because it was something different to what we usually do. It was difficult especially trying to understand what the job in hand was. If I didn't understand what to do there was always someone there within the group who did understand some of the problems.

'I gained lots of knowledge in the things that we did and I gained experience of doing something new. I found the pendulum one boring because it took a long time to solve. In fact we could have had a lot more interesting problems to solve.'

PAULINE

'I found it difficult to do the experiments because I found the instructions difficult to understand. I found it easy to crack the code, but Danny did most of it.

'I liked to work with other students, not on my own but sometimes I found it boring because I could not do it.'

BARRY

'I enjoyed all what went on because it was different to what we have been doing. It was fun.

'Working with the chemicals I found quite difficult. I got the chemicals contaminated and had to do it again. I found though that working in a small group is better for me because if I got stuck there was always someone in the group to help me. I was able to add my ideas to the investigations.

'I gained some skills that I never had before and found it a real challenge for me. I learnt to work in a group and with new people. I also learnt to be more independent. I like being independent.'

MARK

'I liked doing the project with Tony. I liked doing all the puzzles that Tony and Ray set up for us. I think my favourite puzzle was the one where we had to see if we could make a pendulum swing 44 times in a minute. Tony said that I did very well when I was on my own without the rest of my group who were at swimming or movement.

'I liked working in my group and solving the puzzles. I found that if I got stuck or mixed up in what I was saying or doing, the rest of my group were there to help me. There was three people in my group at the start and I think that was the right number of people. It was enjoyable because I get on well with people. However, near the end, Pauline and Krister came and joined the group. I think if Krister had worked with Nicky she would have learnt more. I wasn't sure that Pauline learnt a lot either because she didn't fully understart what we were doing. I knew this because after everything that we did, she kept on asking questions. I think everything happened a bit too quick for Pauline and Krister to take it all in and Krister had no way of telling me or Daniel or Barry to slow down because she never uses her bliss book unless she works with Nicky. Nicky understands everything Krister says. I felt that we were let down towards the end of the project because Pauline and Krister weren't in our group when we first started. Our group was the largest at the end. If our group had stayed as it was from the start I think we would have got a lot more out of the Project.

'There was really only one thing that I found difficult and that was when the group solved a puzzle and Tony gave us an envelope and inside the flap there was a clue as to where the treasure was to be found. In order to look for the treasure you had to crack the code that was written on the flap of the envelope. I found this bit of the project difficult.

'I was happy with the way everying was except for the fact that our group kept getting larger with Krister and Pauline starting the Project late. I felt we had to keep back tracking and explaining to them what we were doing. I felt that this took up a lot of our useful time.'

Teacher evaluation

A teacher at School A

In my school there has been the desire to implement more co-operative, active, investigatory and discovery orientated learning styles. This desire relates not just to any innate advantages or desirability of more flexible learning and teaching styles, but also to the personal and interpersonal needs of pupils at the school in relation to such approaches.

The threat to personal confidence and self esteem posed by investigatory and discovery orientated learning styles is problematic. The pupils at the school, because of their fragile and frequently chaotic emotional make-up, tend to need the security afforded by firm structure; sharply defined boundaries; easily distinguished expectations; clear criteria for assessment. Hence their placement in a special school operating a behaviour modification system.

This does not mean that more flexible approaches are not possible but that the careful management of such is vital if pupils are to have positive learning experiences and not ones that 'set up' or 'create' situations which generate feelings of insecurity and anxiety and which may reinforce images and past experiences of personal failure in coping. Likewise, in the interpersonal realm, relationships tend to deteriorate and become antagonistic or confrontational very quickly. Consequently co-operative working is difficult for pupils and requires sensitive management and support. Paradoxically the need for successful co-operative working experiences is highly desirable as a way of helping pupils face up to and work at resolving interpersonal difficulties.

Project Treasure Hunt provides an opportunity to engage in flexible and co-operative learning situations within a clearly structured programme, having clear parameters and purpose. From the pupils' point of view the project enables flexibility without threat of failure. The emphasis is very much on positive experiences of success through encouraging pupils to be more independent and in control of their own learning, and as such has been a therapeutic as well as an educational experience.

The project offers a way of building confidence and expertise for staff who are non-science specialists, in setting up, managing and assessing practical work, using very limited resources. Class teachers at the school have to teach their groups and as non-specialists there has tended to be an over emphasis on theoretical knowledge related to textbook content. It has helped develop confidence and expertise in meeting the demands of National Curriculum Attainment Target 1.

It is considered that Project Treasure Hunt has a crucial developmental role to play in meeting pupil needs and experiences in learning within science and in meeting broader curriculum demands being made of the nature and emphasis of science teaching by class teachers. This project has acted as both a stimulus and as a catalyst for addressing the issues related to practical science and associated investigatory methodology.

The most important phase will be how the 'lessons' learnt by the pupils and teachers participating in the project can be disseminated through the school. The project is not viewed as an end in itself but rather as an initiatory phase of a potential programme for whole staff and curriculum development.

A teacher at School B

Much of the science work I have been involved with at my school has relied on the teacher being the knowledge base. Although some lessons focused on experiential science, much of the work was from a theoretical base. I wanted to allow the students to experiment but due to the physical difficulties that each had, this form of science was problematic. Working in small groups alleviated some of the problems as this allowed pupils to support one another within this type of lesson structure. There were nevertheless pupils who did not participate due to lack of coordination; lack of previous knowledge; lack of motivation; problems associated with little understanding of scientific concepts.

This project has introduced us to an alternative form of science lesson structure. It has taken the form of science experimentation through problem solving and code breaking.

Each problem area was a separate work station which covered the physical and chemical areas of science. A system could be devised to encompass the biological aspects as well. I was unaware of how successful this form of science would be for our students but decided to give it a try.

The groups consisted of three groups of three students of mixed ability at the start. Two other students joined the class towards the end of the project. Once the stations were set up, groups could choose what they wished to do first.

Having a problem to solve engendered a real enthusiasm and motivation for pupils to get involved. The system proved so successful that pupils had to be ordered to stop at the end of the lesson otherwise they would have kept going and missed their bus home.

Groups were using scientific principles unknowingly. Their recordings were methodical and everyone was involved. No pupil was left out to sit and observe as they all wanted to participate.

I was astounded at how well they had tackled this science work. Everyone in the science class looked forward to the next science lesson with eagerness. Clearly this is a positive move forward for science in my school and is an encouraging source for further experimentation. This type of approach to science could be modified for younger pupils in the school.

The work was safe, especially for the students in wheelchairs. We did not use any hazardous chemicals. The acid used was citric acid and other chemicals used did not present any safety risk. All of the investigations that were performed required very basic scientific apparatus and we did not need the use of a specialist science laboratory area, although we did need a sink and supply of water.

This type of scientific experimentation will form part of our future science programme and hopefully will be used with younger pupils in the school. The groups who were involved in this project were in Years 9, 10, 11.

Analysis of evaluations

Eleven categories of criteria were identified for the evaluations, e.g. 'enjoyment', 'degree of difficulty'. In the case of the student evaluations, a performance rating was calculated with respect to each category. This was based on a performance continuum using a four-point scale. An example of this is as follows: Category (iv): 'different to normal science' – very different (4); different (3); same as normal (2); worse than normal (1).

The results are presented in Table 7.1. The teacher evaluation was based on both written and verbal responses made to similar criteria categories, but including three relating to teacher performance. The results are presented in Table 7.2.

Discussion

The student performance ratings and teacher evaluation can be summarised as follows:

1. Practical work was a great motivator for the students. Both sets of students had limited experience of practical work and were keen to experience extended practical work. The problem solving methodology contained within this practical work was very different to that which they were used to in their normal science lessons.

2. Problem solving allowed the students to take responsibility for their learning by encouraging them to organise themselves within their groups into adopting specific roles, in order to help them solve a particular problem and achieve a desired outcome. They came up with their own strategies. Collaboration was evident throughout. The code breaking strategy was seen to be transferred from activity to activity with relative ease, once students had identified the process involved. However there is little or no evidence to suggest that the students will transfer such a problem solving process to general or everyday situations, which is not surprising given the nature of the project and the time spent on it. However the student/ teacher evaluations suggest that both groups of students were certainly more aware of their capability to solve problems of the type encountered.

3. Both sets of students needed help in handling equipment and in utilising basic numeracy and literacy skills. It was evident that some prior knowledge was also important if the students were to understand the nature of the activity that they were encountering. (It is important that the students can gain access into each activity initially and that teachers then adopt an intervention as opposed to instruction methodology in order to help enhance student thinking and promote the use of more advanced reasoning skills.) Thus, rather than adopting a 'do', 'try', 'make', type approach, the teacher, where necessary, adopted a 'how', 'why', 'what', methodology. This subtle difference in approach put the emphasis firmly back with the students to think about their thinking, which was to help them to come up with successful strategies.

4. Both sets of students found that the tasks were difficult, but not beyond their capability since they all discovered the location of the treasure eventually. It was important that sufficient time was made available for this in order to enable them to discuss their strategies, make and test predictions and repeat or redesign their plans. As the students gained more experience of the activities, with the emphasis on talk and listening to one another, so their confidence seemed to grow. This was especially evident amongst students from School B.

5. The students themselves felt that they had achieved much from the

Table 7.1 Summary of student evaluation. Performance ratings

Category	Range of performance	School A (n = 7)	School B (n = 9)	Comments
[i] group work/interaction	very important – better on own	63%	96%	Some conflict observed during activity sessions especially with School A students
[ii] enjoyment	very enjoyable – boring	69%	93%	The term 'boring' had to be decoded and put into the context within which the student was using it
[iii] practical work	very good – disappointing	100%	89%	Here practical work includes 'the doing' AND 'the thinking' that occurred
[iv] problem-solving approach	very good – disappointing	100%	82%	This relates to the actual activities and not the code breaking activities
[v] code breaking	very interesting – boring	100%	88%	
[vi] different to normal science	very different – worse than normal	100%	96%	Students were asked to compare this to their normal everyday science that they had been studying throughout their schooling.

[vii] type of reward (the hidden treasure = a pen)	very good – disappointing	44%	100%	Many school A students preferred some form of food as the reward.
[viii] help needed	no help – much help	56%	54%	This relates to basic 'handling' skills and assistance with literacy and numeracy skills. Some decoding had to be made from responses.
[ix] recording results	enjoyable – boring	69%	75%	Some students could not read and write due to the nature of their disability.
[x] degree of difficulty	easy – very hard	50%	46%	This relates to the activities and code breaking and NOT to the problems with basic skills although difficult to isolate from responses
[xi] learning occurred	much – nothing new	56%	79%	Students asked to consider this within context of whole project and their evaluation of the project

Table 7.2 Teacher evaluation

Category	Teacher School A	Teacher School B
Interaction/group work	Good. Much cooperation and sharing of ideas/roles. Some care needs to be given to groupings.	Very good. Much cooperation. The students were used to working in groups as normal practice.
Enjoyment	All students enjoyed the project. Some were disappointed with the prize at the completion.	Students enjoyed it. They always looked forward to next lesson. They did not want it to end.
Practical work	Highly motivating. Students had a need to be helped with literacy, numeracy and handling skills.	Motivating. A variety of skills were needed initially for them to access into the task.
Problem solving methodology	Very motivating. Different roles adopted to help solve problems. Students in control of this.	Motivating. Much collaboration. Able to use own ideas/strategies. All achieved some input.
Different to normal science	Very different. Usually more based on theory. Approach to be applied to future lessons.	Very different. More successful than expected. Has implications for future work.
Help needed	Help with basic skills necessary. The emphasis was on helping students to think about strategies.	Help in handling equipment. Some help needed to get students to think about problem.
Recording results	All attempted to record something. The prepared sheets helped. No one disliked this aspect.	All attempted to record through group collaboration. Students organised themselves to do this.
Degree of difficulty	Activities stretched students. Some activities more difficult than others for certain students.	Activities were difficult but all managed to achieve outcomes.
Evidence of learning	Students' self esteem raised but difficult to assess improved science knowledge/understanding.	Using evidence to make their own conclusions. Predicting and testing outcomes.
Teacher/student interaction	Good. Students appreciated help with basic skills as it helped them solve problems.	Excellent. Student/teacher worked together in form of partnership. Both learning from each other.
Teacher expectation	Increased. Both teacher and the student more aware of capability.	Increased. Now know what they can achieve and some of the drawbacks
Teacher confidence	Increased as Project continued. No longer wary of practical work. Support still needed.	Confidence boosted. Approach will form basis of future science.

project and from the process of self-evaluation. They were all very eoloquent when evaluating their work, either verbally or in written form. One particular student was very damning when reporting on another member of the group. This student was able to verbalise his emotions quite succinctly, yet had been unable to do this in the past according to his teacher. Both student and teacher felt that much positive interaction had occurred between them. The notion of a partnership was expressed by the teacher from School B. However it was difficult to assess by the end of the project whether there had been any actual enhancement of science knowledge and understanding.

6. It was found useful to prepare pre-printed sheets with which to allow the students space to record observations, results and make conclusions. The students enjoyed recording their findings, and their recorded results and observations provided the focus for them to analyse and make sense of their investigations.

7. The teachers' expectations of the students' capability has been increased through this project. It is to he hoped that this expectation will be extended into other domains.

8. Teacher confidence has been increased with respect to the teaching of science, utilising a problem-solving methodology through practical work. None of the teachers involved in the project was science trained. However it remains to be seen if this confidence can be continued within future different contexts or whether this confidence has just emanated through the novelty value of the project. This confidence may also be related to the presence of a science trained teacher working alongside them, offering advice and support to both teacher and student.

Further analysis of the performance ratings suggest that for categories [i], [ii], [vii] and [xi] (Table 7.1) there is a marked difference in response between the sets of students from each school.

For instance, some of the students used the word 'boring' to describe one or two of the activities. Perhaps for them the activities were 'boring'. However such comments may more realistically relate to great personal difficulty in concentration which some of the activities tended to highlight.

Some students from School A had a tremendous need to be 'gratified' quickly in terms of an activity being completed or rewarded. As such the requirement of *'disciplined' repetition and recording as part of an investigation, delayed, for an unsatisfactory length of time, the reward of achieving a given outcome'*, as observed by the teacher from School A. This situation was not apparent with students from School B.

Again there was some disappointment from students from School A with the final treasure (a pen). Most wanted some form of food instead. This may further reinforce the need for nurture and gratification.

School B students were used to working with each other in group situations, whereas school A students tended to work individually and independent of each other prior to the project. Problems of conflict between group members did arise in both schools, but were of a more serious nature with school A students. However such problems were the exception rather than the rule. As the teacher from school A further observed, *'interpersonal relationships between pupils throughout the project were generally good with much co-operation and sharing of ideas and role responsibilities'*.

The conflict that arose among School B students only became apparent through the student evaluation stage of the project. One student made it clear that all was going well until two new class members were asked to join the group. This student observed *'Our group got bigger near the end because Krister and Pauline joined. I felt that we had to keep on back tracking and explaining to them what we were doing. I felt that this took up a lot of our useful time'*.

This was the only evidence of any apparent conflict among School B students. This particular student went on to reaffirm his frustration of this through further discussion, but this frustration was not evident during the actual practical session.

Conclusion

The limited evidence obtained through observation of the students working on each problem-solving activity and listening to their self-evaluations of the work, seems to support the description for Active Learners outlined by Bentley and Watts (1989).

The problem-solving activities and the notion of a treasure hunt appears to have acted as the motivator in enabling the students to decide and satisfy their own knowledge needs.

The descriptors for Active Learners were in evidence albeit in a qualitative way, in that students took responsibility for their learning through shared ownership of what they were doing with the teachers, and in so doing became highly motivated during the process. This is evident in the self-evaluations made by the students, although one may question the reliability of these.

What is clear from this small scale trial is that all pupils found areas in which they could succeed, by their own definition and in which they could appreciate the contributions of others. Furthermore it would appear that most of the students realised or became more aware of their capability for problem solving. Certainly the teachers were more aware of this by the end of the project.

Whether the original aims of this project have been satisfied or met completely in the short term, is open to interpretation. However the students themselves are shrewd judges of effective teaching and learning approaches. For our purposes the comments from the students, particularly when qualified by the teacher, is strong evidence as to the success of a problem-solving approach.

Observations of the teachers and a review of teacher evaluation tend to indicate that they did emerge as Active Learners themselves. In both schools the teachers found that they were having to change their role and function in order to manage the classroom situation and allow the students to take on more responsibility for their learning. This was no easy task for them, but nevertheless the teachers were prepared to indulge in something new, and had the courage to try out this approach despite the fact that they were aware that mistakes would be made.

Whether the teachers would repeat the exercise or a similar exercise independently remains to be seen. Hopefully this will beneficially affect their vision, planning techniques and classroom roles in the future.

CHAPTER EIGHT

Bright ideas

Di Bentley and Samantha Bentley, Roehampton Institute

This chapter examines issues for students of 'marked aptitude' (Robertson, 1991). It focuses first on some general aspects for teachers in dealing with such students in classrooms and then examines the particular role which problem solving can play in assisting 'bright' or very able students to achieve their full potential, and what teachers need to do to enable this in the classroom.

Strategies for 'bright' pupils

High attainers have always been a thorny problem in the teaching profession. The demise of selective education brought the introduction of comprehensive education in 1965 when, for some teachers, all students were to be treated as seemingly equal, when 'streaming' became a thing of the past, and when any attempt to deal with issues of able students – by doing anything other than ignore them – was frowned upon. But as the saying goes 'what goes around comes around' and during the mid 1970s, Her Majesty's Inspectorate began to alert the profession to the need for attention to such students. Their 1978 survey, for example, stated: 'In the case of the most able groups, the work was considerably less well matched than for average and less able groups.'

However, one of the major problems associated with very able students is how to identify them as a group. It may be that, as Robertson states, we can only identify them accurately through aptitudes in particular curriculum areas. Later in this chapter we examine those aspects of science which might be associated with students of marked aptitude.

As the decade progressed, the situation appears to have changed little. Bennett *et al.* in 1984 were still saying: 'High attainers were underestimated on 40% of the tasks assigned to them.' And HMI as recently as 1992 stated: 'In the majority of schools the expectations for very able pupils are not sufficiently high.'

It is interesting to compare the euphemisms used for such students by different groups. From 'marked aptitude' (Robertson, 1991) through 'high attainers' to 'very able', no group of writers seems able to agree on a classification for students who require a high level of support and autonomy such as these. Nor, officially, are they identified within government funding structures as having 'special educational needs'. Even the recent changes brought about in the assessment and management of Special Educational Needs (SEN) by the 1993 Education Act have ignored such students. This is despite the fact that the policy statements on SEN from several local education authorities indicate that the spectrum of special needs includes everything from the designated Warnock categories (Warnock, 1993) to the most able. Evidence from a variety of sources seems to suggest that students who are in the category of 'very able' are frequently those who might display behavioural difficulties and 'hyperactivity'. Certainly IQ tests by Cohen and Taylor (1972) on category A prisoners in the 1970s indicates that a far higher proportion of these people are in the high IQ range than would be indicated simply by chance. It appears that one of the few ways that very able students can be granted funding for much needed extra help under the 1981 Education Act is to be categorised as having Emotional and Behavioural Difficulties (EBD). Otherwise, simply being of marked aptitude does not qualify students for extra resources, however much they may need them.

Given that this is the case, what can teachers do who find themselves faced with the need to cater within a mixed-ability situation for the needs of high achievers? Eyre (1993) suggests that five possibilities are usually posed. She regards these to be:

- a separate programme of work decided upon by the teacher for the child;
- additional or supplementary work sometimes to be done at home;
- the child working for some time with older children;
- the child to be withdrawn from the class for small group work;
- acceleration to a higher class.

She acknowledges the point that all of these solutions require access to resources that very often are not available. She states that what is needed is: 'an approach in schools which routinely provides challenge for the most able pupils; especially if we are to provide for pupils who show a marked aptitude in one subject'.

We believe that problem solving as a learning approach in the curriculum of every class meets the needs she describes. Gagne pointed out as long ago as 1970 that:

> 'When problem solution is achieved, something is also learned, in the sense that the individual's capability is more or less permanently changed. . . . Problem solving, then, must definitely be considered a form of learning.'

Problem solving encourages students to work together and develop their creativity and understanding in a learning approach which allows full reign to the developing cognition of the child. As Johnsey(1986) states:

> 'Making decisions about the solution of a problem is a creative activity and often the end product will be expression of the child's personality. . . . We must use our skills as teachers to set problems which stretch the imagination of the child but at the same time lie within her/his sphere of ability.'

The role of problem solving

But why is problem solving so suitable for the more able students, apart from its ability to differentiate by outcome? Watts (1991) gives some examples of skills and states that problem solving is a 'higher order skill' (p.13). In providing access to such higher order skills, teachers can allow more able students to exercise their own autonomy, seek their own solutions and thereby develop their own cognitive skills more fully. It is this development of autonomy and the opportunity to explore previously unknown areas in depth which provides much of the source of enjoyment for pupils of marked aptitude. In general, teachers use a variety of problem solving approaches in their science classrooms, but these are most frequently of the 'constrained' or teacher based type of problems. Rarely are students allowed a fairly free range at a problem of their own choosing or design. Still more rarely are students given the opportunity to tackle fully commercially based problems which have an actual application in the real world and contribute to the work of an industrial company. Better still, which contribute to the furtherance of science as a field of knowledge. In the remainder of the chapter we explore some examples of an area of work where such problems have been the main focus.

Earlier chapters in the book have mentioned the work of the CREST Awards team (for example, CREST, 1992) and we would refer readers to these for further descriptions. In this chapter we are concerned only with a small collection of the work of the scheme – the Gold Awards. It is work at this level, with its implications for partnership between industry and schools, that provides the greatest stimulus for the development of students of marked aptitude. The CREST Award scheme requires students at Gold level to identify and work on their own problems. These problems are identified through an 'active partnership' between the students or school and the industrial/business community.

The nature of the problem-solving process places considerable emphasis on 'problem identification', 'negotiation' and links between the student or school and a range of outside agencies. Students are encouraged to develop their own strategies and are allowed to experience the successes (and failures) associated with project management. Students negotiate their progress and assessment with an attached industrialist, and it is this guidance which assists them in achieving what they need in pursuit of their project objectives. Some 800 Gold Award projects were registered with CREST in the 1992/93 year, and the majority of this work has taken place in the post-16 phase of education. The nature of the education system in Britain is such that by far the greatest concentration of students of marked aptitude are, by reason of the selectivity of the system, to be found in the post -16 phase, usually engaged in an A-level course.

Examining statistics published by the Department for Education for A-level (DFE, 1993) indicate that the great majority of the students are male. This implies then that groups of A-level students will be comprised solely of males in many instances. Certainly this is borne out by an analysis of those projects which were presented at the CREST Gold Awards ceremonies in 1992 and 1993 (CREST, 1992, 1993). Table 8.1 below shows the breakdown of this information. It is clear that in problem-solving terms, there are far fewer girls than boys and, in general, girls prefer to work in groups rather than alone. Boys, on the other hand, are a little more inclined to work with other boys than work alone, and only a quarter of them work in groups with girls.

Inevitably such data regarding boys and girls working together must be interpreted with caution, since the majority of the schools entering students for awards at Gold level are single-sex schools. What the data does make clear is that girls in general prefer not to work alone. This is

Table 8.1 Analysis of CREST Gold Awards by year and gender of working group

	1992	1993
Total number of projects	42	43
Percentage of projects with both boys and girls	24	26
Percentage of girls only	19	26
Percentage of boys only	57	51
Percentage of boys working alone	40	35
Percentage of girls working alone	2	14

Table 8.2 CREST Gold Awards 1992/93, categorised by nature of project investigated, and by gender of working group

Project category	Gender of students completing project		
	Boys	Girls	Boys and girls
Computers	3	3	0
Safety	1	2	3
Health	3	2	2
Measurement	2	1	1
Environment	1	2	1
Human interest	4	1	1
Scientific theory	3	1	1

in keeping with a great deal of the work on gender in schools whcih has been researched over the last decade. It is an important point in the nature of designing work for students of marked aptitude.

What is of greater interest, however, is the nature of the problems chosen by students. There is a great deal of information, much of it stemming from the work of the Assessment of Performance Unit (APU, 1989) concerning students' liking and understanding of concepts in science. Much of this data shows stereotypic trends in terms of preference of activity between boys and girls. The data for the Gold Awards shows a different picture, however. In general, categorisation of projects over 1992/3 showed the given results in Table 8.2.

Obviously not all of the 85 projects in Table 8.1 are illustrated here: many were single-subject categories and so analysis of the data in this way would be meaningless. What this rough analysis does show, however, is that boys and girls are equally interested in solving those problems which might have been considered to be 'girl friendly', and thus attract the attention of those few girls who do take A-level sciences. Several of the projects, for example, might be seen to come within a category of 'human interest' – such as designing tools for handicapped persons, an electronic child-finder, and music therapy research. A 'scientific theory' category might include research into carbon 60 , work on genetics and chaos theory. At least one student is in the process of publication of his work in a scientific journal.

What then does this tell us about what teachers might do to prepare for teaching 'gifted' or 'bright' pupils? First there are issues about the nature of the work. The Gold Awards data seems to indicate that the type of problem is not vital. Students will choose across a variety of fields, including those that seem to be, at first sight, not particularly interesting. Nor are such choices necessarily gender related. What does seem to be important from the CREST Gold Awards experience is that able students need both autonomy and support: autonomy to work and make mistakes and develop their ideas and understandings and, indeed, in terms of some of scientific theory work, they need the understandings of others. Support from real experts in the field is necessary so that their own ideas can be challenged and developed and their work related to real situations. The CREST experience indicates that this is when teachers take a back seat – they become facilitators, fixers who arrange for outside expertise. They then nourish this, keep it going and act as a go-between for students and their industrial mentors.

The working arrangements for boys and girls, however, do seem to be important. Girls seem to prefer sharing and collaborating in problem solving, whereas many boys are more happy to work alone. The assessment criteria for the Gold Awards draw attention to the collaborative nature of problem solving and this would seem to give girls a definite advantage. What is obvious, however, is that many of the more able students will have experiences of science education where they have been relatively isolated individuals, with little access to stimulating ideas from peers at their own level. Collaborative problem solving is a definite advantage under these circumstances since it exposes students to challenge and critique, sharpens and hones their thinking and develops the social skills and team-work that they will need as future scientists. An interesting side reflection here, however, is that in the category of the development of 'aspects of scientific theory', all but one of the projects were developed by individuals.

Recognising students of marked aptitude and providing for them

How do teachers recognise students of marked aptitude? There are the obvious ways – these are the students who achieve the highest marks and/or display the most enthusiasm for an area of work. They are also the most original thinkers and thus in many respects may be the most threatening to teach. All of us at some time in our teaching lives have taught students whose intellect we have respected as being greater than our own and we have recognised our limitations in providing them with the challenging conditions needed to keep them actively learning. Our contention here is that problem-solving activities provide precisely the conditions that such students need. In providing problem-solving opportunities, we suggest teachers need to organise the '5 E' additives:

- *Expertise* for students, which comes from access to applied and theoretical science, and which is invested in sources other than the teacher.
- *Experience* of skills necessary to solve problems, from team-work to scientific process, in sufficient quantities to allow thinking to develop and be questioned.
- *Exposure* to the theories and ideas of others such as their peers and practising scientists through their original writings.
- *Explanations* and interpretations of ideas and possible solutions to problems.
- *Examination* of the results and solutions by students and others so that reformulation or refinement can take place.

And, finally, what skills will students have after experience of problem solving? Evidence from the Gold Awards shows that such students are more confident, more assured of what they know, eager to share and extend their skills of explanation, concerned for accuracy, insightful, and collaborative. They are better at listening to advice and acting on it and unafraid to question when they are uncertain or when they disagree. They can also see the relationships between theory and practice much more clearly and have the capacity to be innovative and take risks in trying out solutions. Is this not what we would want of the most able students in the next generation? In our view, problem solving can achieve all this, and so we would want to add a sixth to our five ways to cater for the needs of able children, this sixth for use in mixed-ability situations. It is an adage outlined by Eyre (1993):

'All children and especially those of marked aptitude should have a regular diet of open-ended, learner-centred problem solving in all aspects of their curriculum.'

CHAPTER NINE

Cases of teaching teachers for problem solving

Steve Alsop and Mike Watts, Roehampton Institute

Problems with problem solving

'It might be fun to do yourself but it's no fun trying to organise pupils to do it.'

It is not unusual for teachers to enjoy the processes of problem solving but to shrink from the implementation of problem solving in the classroom. In this chapter we explore several different ways in which we have, over time, managed to involve teachers and trainee teachers, inducting them into problem-solving activities for use in schools. Our purpose has been to initiate them into the skills and outcomes they want from children in their classes.

There is an informal division amongst all of those teachers we know. Some will find almost any reason that moves in order not to innovate with open-ended problem solving ('It wouldn't work in my school'; 'You couldn't do it with my class'; 'My Head won't like it'; 'The head of department wouldn't let me do it' etc.). On the other hand, there are those teachers who manage to undertake (insist upon!) some excellent work in innovative ways *despite* the difficulties (lack of resources, unwilling colleagues, unpromising pupils, poor support, etc.). Those teachers in the first group may be people who find experimentation risky and difficult and look to a range of external constraints as plausible obstacles to having to innovate. Those in the second group are probably natural risk takers and feed their innovative urges through tackling new teaching approaches regardless of the difficulties. Possibly because of the difficulties.

On the whole, those who reject such an open-ended way of working do so for a number of plausible reasons. These include the following.

Heavily constrained curriculum time

In the current educational climate in the UK, schools are working to very tight syllabuses, which are very prescriptive in nature. Increasingly, lesson time is allocated in terms of curriculum topics which are fused with the National Curriculum (NCC, 1991a, b) statements of attainment. Within this context, curriculum time is at a premium and must heavily influence teachers' choices of pedagogical approach. For many teachers, problem solving is perceived as a leisurely pursuit which consumes valuable teaching time. We talked to Vanessa, a recently qualified teacher, who told us:

> 'After I had been given a massive syllabus, and every lesson was crammed full of content, problem solving appeared an awful waste of time'.

Planning and organisation

Problem-solving activities require more organisation beyond the usual practical activities. Many of these organisational factors have been listed in Watts (1991), namely:

- Trying to guess what kind of special apparatus or material children will need.
- Getting hold of a large amount of consumable items like string, sellotape, scissors, glue, cardboard and so on.
- Predicting what text and visual material will be needed to stimulate ideas.
- Designing 'clue cards', safety instructions, pre-reading, homework etc.
- Planning the timing, technical support, room layout, disposal of waste; planning the teachers' change of role.
- Selecting tools that are appropriate in size and kind; are they in good condition, and easily available? Are all work surfaces suitable? Have safety procedures been established for access and use of the tools?

There are many other considerations. For example, one approach is to require the pupils to order their own materials. This has obvious difficulties, since it requires pupils to be aware of the school's or department's ordering system which, in turn, must be very robust and prepared to put up with the idiosyncratic nature of some pupils' orders. We recall an incident, in a science lesson, when a group of youngsters had been set the rather innocuous task of 'testing the strength of paper bags'. Each group was requested to make an order for the materials and equipment they required. We scrutinised their requests before passing the orders on to the technical staff. At the end of a list of 'paper, Newton metres, sellotape, clamp stand', we noticed, in small handwriting, 'Van de Graaf Generator'. When questioned the group claimed that 'they saw it at the back of the room and thought it might come in handy!'

A general lack of resources and materials, including technical support

It follows from what has been said that problem solving can require a large array of resources, equipment and materials. These have to be maintained and this can be an extra strain on already overworked technical support.

A perceived loss of control

The very nature of problem solving requires that children be granted considerable levels of autonomy. This requires the class teacher to adopt a range of pedagogical approaches that facilitate pupil autonomy. These approaches may be different to those commonly employed by the teacher, and be seen to be risky on a number of counts. Many teachers associate the reduction in their 'delivery' of the curriculum with a reduction in their classroom control and discipline. In this context open ended work is seen as a recipe for disaster with certain demanding groups. These feelings are typified by comments of the kind:

> 'I have enough difficulties keeping Year 8 seated, let alone getting them to behave when they are performing open ended problem solving activities; problem solving is like letting the lid off a can of worms.'

Loss of control over the learned content

As noted in Chapter 1, many teachers associate children's learning with their own 'delivery' of subject content: 'They won't know it unless I *tell* it to them'. Given this framework, it is not surprising that the process of handing over the responsibility for the 'learning' to the 'learner' entails a worrying loss of control over the learned content. This anxiety is characterised by comments of the kind: 'how can I be sure in problem solving that they have learnt the right thing? It is too much like them just playing – they are not using the right thought processes. It's just trial and error'.

National Curriculum cross-curricular skills and dimensions

A single impetus for the use of problem solving in classrooms is its explicit and implicit requirement within the National Curriculum both for science and technology. This is dealt with in part in other chapters. We need mention here only that teacher education is intimately concerned with ensuring that teachers and trainee teachers are fully familiar with these requirements. Problem solving is a cluster of skills which principally devolve responsibility for decision making to the pupils and lead them to shape the direction of their own solutions. This is evident in the investigative and 'process' components of science and in much of the central cycle of activities in technology.

In this sense, problem solving is something to be experienced in practice as well as discussed at a theoretical level. Teachers need to know what potential the approach has for developing pupils' skills while at the same time considering the implication for conceptual development, motivation, attitudinal change and manipulative skills, and how to set about it in the classroom.

Our approach to teacher education: theory and practice, thought and action

'I want them (trainee teachers) to concentrate on classroom skills rather than academic training. I'm interested in real children, in real classrooms, not academic theory'.
(Kenneth Clarke, then Secretary of State for Education, LEA Conference, Southport, 4th January, 1992)

The current culture in the politics of education is that theory is seen to have little bearing on classrooms, that the teaching of children in 'real classrooms' relies upon a set of eclectic and pragmatic skills rather than theoretically informed action. It appears to be frowned upon for teachers to have 'academic training' in ways that would detract from the 'realities' of classroom life. For us, then, this might be a good time to write about theory. This is not just a reactionary perversity but a wish to re-affirm the value of having a theoretical framework through which to view educational issues.

In our view, teacher education proceeds through cycles of conceptualisation, experiential learning, tactical evaluation and professional reflection. In fact, through a 'designer version' of the problem solving cycle itself, where the cycle itself is designed for the particular

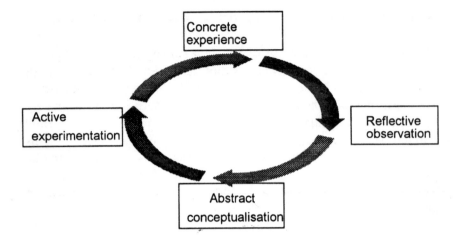

Figure 9.1

needs of the classroom practitioners. This 'professional problem solving' trades on both a theoretical perspective of teaching and learning and the appreciation of the practical application of the teaching and learning involved. It is an experiential learning cycle of the sort outlined by Gibbs (1988) based on Kolb's (1984) theories on experience as the basis for learning and development. This cycle is illustrated in Figure 9.1. As usual, there are questions as to whether this is a cycle, a continuous spiral of processes or whether they are all present and happening at the same time. The key point here for us that learners have some basis for their reflections – a baseline of evidence that is not just theoretical but has a foundation in concrete experience.

This cycle relates to our work in problem solving since it neatly describes the sort of experiences we try to develop with teachers and student teachers. There are times we have began with the 'abstract conceptualisation' and talked though some of the cognitive and intellectual skills problem solvers need to exhibit, their motivation and attitude changes. This has then set a frame within which they have designed and run an experiment in school with children, or engineered activities with themselves as learners. They have engaged in 'concrete experiences' in the pursuit of solutions to problems at their own level and then spent a period of time in reflective observation with the resulting outcomes. At other times we have started the cycle elsewhere and thrown them straight into the concrete experience with the edict that they must operate at least at two levels – 'hands on' task and 'heads on' processes.

There are arguments, of course that this is not a cycle at all and that the process of conceptualisation, concrete experience, experimentation and reflection can all happen at the same time and there is no need for them to follow one another in sequence. We would accept that this can be the case. However, we have used the cycle both as a description of some individuals' actions as well as a means of structuring activities for teachers.

Hands-on concrete experience

Before moving on it is worth delving a little further into the need for physical experience in problem solving. It is our belief that there is always a need for active manipulation or exploration of a situation: a 'conversation' between the problem solver and the immediate problem environment. Such a conversation can stem from playfulness, curiosity or some intriguing event, and results in the problem solver interacting physically with the problem situation. Indeed, Woolnough and Allsop (1985) maintain that this is a vital ingredient to science itself:

> 'The art, and the craft, of a scientist can only be developed through practical hands-on experience. Experience is also a necessary precursor to understanding the theoretical concepts behind a phenomenon, and can give reality to models and theories after they have been introduced.'

Sometimes 'hands-on' activity can reveal a solution to a problem quite easily, at other times it has to be discovered by a detailed and time-consuming examination of the situation. For the ultimate solution of a practical task, both patience and a good economy might be needed. Past experience will determine whether or not a particular situation will be seen as a problem or not. It will also determine the range of situation that are seen to be problematic, and the experiences where the solver can begin to 'get into' the problem at all (without having to call for expert help). It is determined by motivation and personal interest – some people are more ready to 'have a go' than others: some are willing to engage in activity in a large number of areas and so their experiences become richer and they more opportunities to solve more problems of different types. That is, different problems mean different things to different people at different times.

It is interesting to divert for a moment and consider a very particular aspect to 'hands-on' for problem solving – the use of drawings. As Larkin (1980) points out, even expert problem solvers need to draw pictures as they solve problems. This might seem surprising, since experts might be expected to carry their thinking in their heads without need to draw a sketch. This is probably because most people assume that using a diagram or a picture makes a problem clearer: external representation aids internal representation. An expert might be expected to need no help with internalised pictures since solving problems in the head might be seen as an indication of what it is to be an expert.

Many learners need to draw as they work, not scale diagrams but symbolic sketches. The general feeling is that this different kind of 'conversation' with paper and pencil helps to summarise the problem, suggest projected solutions, shapes planning and possible divisions of labour. A drawing, too, allows for parallel representations. It can code several aspects of the problem at the same time. Speech is linear and different parts of the discussion can become separated by several sentences or by minutes of time as one participant describes possible ways forward to another. This can overload the conversational system and a drawing then can summarise several features all at once.

Before we begin to tackle some examples of these issues further, we want to ruminate on the distinction between 'reality' and 'theory' for a moment. In the literature on philosophy and the philosophy of science there are countless theories about what is real and what 'reality' means. This is not the place to recount them all. Similarly there are innumerable books on real (versus unreal, or surreal?) theories and, again, this is not the place to enumerate these. What is lacking in such ill-informed comments as Clarke's observations on education is a sense of balanced insight: that theory and practice go hand in hand, coupled and entangled not divided and distant. Activity without theory is blind, is random and accidental, is simple trial and error. Similarly, theory without 'real' action becomes self-fulfilling, feeding only on itself and becomes monstrously rhetorical. Instead, when the two are balanced, theory teaches us how to do things and offers techniques that solve problems. Theory is a tool to be used – it should neither be dominant nor subverted. The combination of theory and practice means learning by doing.

In our view everyone has theories. Its not just politicians, teacher trainers or teachers, but learners as well. And one of the most exciting areas for exploring youngsters' theories is through their solving of problems. This is where their thoughts meet their solutions, where their ideas encounter their outcomes. This is especially true where the problems are open-ended and task-based, so that the range of possible solutions is wide and the likely results quite varied.

We can now describe some of the instances and circumstances where we have developed these ideas with different client groups.

Some example approaches

Case 1: problem solving with PGCE students

Post Graduate Certificate of Education (PGCE) courses are driven by forces increasingly outside the control of institutes of higher education like our own. We feel keenly, though, that some of the philosophy and practice of active learning in classrooms needs to be brought home to students as they are working on the course. Here we discuss just two examples of the activities we have undertaken in the past.

As teacher trainers we advocate many different teaching methodologies. Amongst these are those associated with open-ended inquiry and problem solving. How a teacher chooses to teach depends ultimately on their own teaching aims and objectives. The setting of lesson aims and objectives is, in itself, a very demanding task. Calderhead (1984) has argued that teachers rarely start their lesson planning by deciding lesson aims and objectives and, rather, they address the problem of how to structure the time and experience of pupils. This is certainly true of trainee teachers. Their lesson aims and objectives are often tacit and only appear when in conversation after a lesson. Early in the course, we set the students a problem solving task with the following aims:

- To emphasise the interrelationship between teaching methodology and lesson aims and objectives. This includes emphasising the importance of starting the planning of lesson by setting aims and objectives.
- To look at the structure of problem solving lessons to include all aspects of classroom management.
- To introduce students to aspects of problem solving with which they are perhaps not so familiar.

In this instance, students are set the task: 'Build a device, using only the materials provided, that will burst a balloon in exactly 2 minutes. You have one hour to complete this task'.

They are provided with a tray of: 2-metre rules, sellotape, string, two G-clamps plus bosses, pins, candles, two balloons, two beakers, plasticine and five drinking straws.

The willingness of students to engage in problems of this nature is usually very praiseworthy. Their solutions have ranged from suspending a balloon above a pin and using the candle to burn through the string (careful experimentation provides the correct distance between the candle and the string) to attaching the balloon to a drinking straw, threading the string through the straw and suspending this across the room. Here, careful experimentation is needed to deduce the appropriate difference in height between the two ends of the string for the balloon and straw to take 2 minutes to travel from the top to the pin at the bottom.

In this example we start with a problem set at the students' own level. This provides a context for discussion. The students are then shown a video of children completing the same tasks in a local school. This part provides an interesting comparison and has led many students to comment on the sophistication of the children's solutions – when starting to teach it is very easy to underestimate the ability of pupils in the class.

Following this, the students are split into different groups and are asked to discuss the following questions:

- In tackling the problem what skills did you bring to the task?
- What do you think of this investigation as a learning activity?
- What did the pupils learn? (the link between learning outcomes and lesson aims is important here);
- How would you organise the classroom/pupils if you were going to do this activity?
- What sort of introduction would you give at the start?
- How would you bring the lesson to a focus at the end?
- How does this activity relate to the National Curriculum?

As the PGCE course progresses, we actively promote problem solving in a range of contexts. So, for example, we have undertaken 'biotechnological' problems with dairy products in conjunction with the Milk Marketing Board; looked at physics problems and 'Newtons Laws on ice' at the local skating rink, and taken (and developed) reasonably good photographs (all of 'still life' subjects!) with pin hole cameras. By exposing trainee teachers to problem solving experiences, we hope they will adopt these as they plan and support their lesson aims and objectives.

Towards the end of the course we ask students to make a five minute video documentary on 'the environment'. This activity provides a framework for actively promoting the use of video approaches in lessons, and it:

- familiarises students with its use;

- enables a detailed look at the cross curricular themes;
- broadens the context of problem solving beyond those usually associated with school science and technology activities.

The production of their own video on environmental issues has also accentuated the processes within problem solving – and has highlighted the evaluative element in particular. There are none so critical as they who must put their outcomes up for a 'showing'!

In all, the processes prompted a range of questions such as: How can we organise the sessions? How do pupils react? How can we split pupils into effective teams and groups? What roles can they play? What are the central classroom management issues? A highlight of one of our ex-student's first year of teaching was a video which a group of her Year 9 pupils made of a science lesson. This was copied and pupils were able to take it home and show their parents/guardians a 'snippet' of their science lesson. In showing the video of children at work they see the enjoyment and enthusiasm, and can then look at the ways of arranging a classroom to maximise this, and how readily children take to this approach.

Case 2: BAQTS Students

The undergraduate course within education that carries Qualified Teacher Status at Roehampton Institute (our BA(QTS) programme), is a course for primary teachers. As part of the course there is a compulsory 'science studies' component, a mini-course of five modules. The modules are designed to extend the 'science strength' of intending primary teachers, and students are required to learn science at their own level. Within the modules we build in some problem solving, and two examples are given here. They are examples of what Munson (1988) calls 'curriculum dedicated' problems, they stem directly from the curricular work in progress at the time.The two we have chosen are of a chemical and biological nature. It has been noted in Watts (1991) that problems in science tend to be of the physics/ technological persuasion; we are redressing the balance by presenting two here that are not:

1. Design and build an electric battery, which will give the highest current. The battery is to be constructed using only the materials likely to be found in the kitchen. You need to be able to connect your battery to an ammeter for judging.
2. Plan and carry out an investigation into an aspect of human

learning. It is recommended that you confine your study to the acquisition of a simple skill or to an aspect of memory.

Many of our students have a limited background in science. The majority will have finished studying science at age 16. Problems of this nature are demanding, their open-endedness often leaves students lacking confidence and unsure of the appropriate starting place. However once they get started their solutions can be highly imaginative. On some occasions the students become so carried away that any sense of a pragmatic approach is cast adrift in favour of the spectacular 'all moving-all dancing solution!'

The kitchen battery is a problem which requires a theoretical starting point. It was used as an activity for students to apply some of the electrochemical content covered in the course. There are a large number of solutions which vary from a modification of a well known approach, a lemon with a piece of tin and copper inserted as electrodes, to the slightly more unorthodox. A copper sauce pan and an aluminium pencil sharper provide two metals which are separated in the electrochemical series, using oven cleaner as the electrolyte produces a single cell. A collection of sauce pans with pencil sharpeners suspended in over cleaner all connected in parallel is actually quite a successful (if ungainly) approach.

Many students find the investigation into human learning difficult. It is necessary to state a testable hypothesis and then design a suitable experiment. The skill of solving a simple maze, cut from cardboard whilst blindfolded, works well. This has been extended to address the following testable hypotheses:

- are girls better than boys at learning the maze;
- are left-handed people better than right handed;
- are dyslexic people better than non-dyslexic;
- are children better than adults at learning the maze?

For some students the open-endedness of the problem provides an irresistible temptation to incorporate a particular skill they have recently mastered and to use this as their test. This was the case when a student decided to base her whole investigation on tap dancing. A group of experienced tap dancers were assembled and set the task of learning a new tap routine. This group was then compared with a group of willing volunteers who had never tap-danced before and were set the same task of learning a new dance routine. Her hypothesis was that 'experienced tap dancers are better at learning tap dances than complete novices.' We leave the conclusion up to your imagination other than to say that, after careful conversation and discussion with us in the lab, she agreed to use the pencil maze. The advantages of using problem solving have been discussed at length in earlier chapters. Once the initial fear of starting the problem is breached it is surprising how even the most pragmatic can become carried away.

Case 3: Involvement in national projects

Because of our work with a number of national projects, we have had the opportunity of inducting new teachers into problem solving activities through funded development work . Foremost of these has been in collaboration with the CREST Award Scheme and through the work of the World Wide Fund for Nature (Edwards, Watts and West, 1993). The CREST Award scheme is a project mentioned several times in other chapters. It is a well-developed and vibrant scheme which is active in many schools nationally and has often made opportunities to induct teachers both into the scheme and the arcane pleasures of problem solving.

There were two parts to the CREST/WWF development work: the preparatory training for an Environmental Award Project, and the publication of some of the results when they emerged. In the early stages, CREST and WWF collaborated to establish an environmental problem solving scheme and entries were submitted by many teachers from all over the country. The induction for the scheme was enacted in two ways – through an initial, central, conference/workshop for all those involved, and through regional seminar/workshops a year later for new entrants to the process. Both approaches were a great success and, again, the 'experiential learning cycle' came to the fore. At both the national conference and regional workshops all the participants were expected to work in teams (away from friends and in cahoots with teachers from other parts of the country) and to actively solve difficult problems. They were expected not just to talk about it (and how it might be done in class) but to actually sort through some of the processes in action. This was not only marvellous fun (full of ingenuity and creativity) but also served to focus discussion marvellously: abstraction and conceptualisation happened alongside an appreciation of the cognitive and manipulative skills required. In some of the regional workshops the problem activities were 'sponsored' by local business and commerce, and representatives of each were there to set up the task, add realism and relevance, and support the team as they worked. Camaraderie, connections, cooperation and colleagueship grew as each working moment passed and the problem solving tasks gave purchase to each part of the discussion and debate.

The resulting skills and motivation were eventually transformed into pupil projects on the environment in and around the schools involved. Some of these are described in Edwards *et al.* (1993) mentioned above. At the latter stages of the project, a group of 'award winning' teachers then came together to report the work of their schools. Again this was an induction into problem solving – in this case the problems of writing and communicating school-based activities. Not all teachers are natural writers and our 'writing-workshop' was an introduction to and realisation of a range of new skills and processes in both individual and 'team' writing. All in all this produced an excellent product and the teachers' tales reflect some creditable work.

Summary

The key part to our work with teachers is to overcome some of the barriers they see to using problem solving in the classroom. We do this – in part – by showing them what are some of the virtues of this way of working for themselves – by putting them through problem-solving exercises. From this experience come a flood of questions, protests, plans and ideas. There is no single formula for the introduction of problem solving in schools and teachers would largely ignore it if there was. Theirs is the task of translating ideas for learning into practice – experimenting with new approaches to see what works best in their own circumstances. We help to generate possible and plausible projects and to show what the priorities and pitfalls are as they work in class. We carry on teaching problem solving because they keep coming back for more.

References

Active Teaching and Learning Approaches in Science Project (1992) Centre for Science Education, Sheffield Hallam University, Sheffield.

Adey, P., Shayer, M. and Yates, C. (1989) *Thinking Science. The curriculum materials of the Cognitive Acceleration through Science Project*. London: Macmillans.

Adey, P., Shayer, M. and Yates, C. (1990) *Better learning: A Report from the Cognitive Acceleration through Science Project*. Centre for Educational Studies, Kings College, University of London.

Assessment of Performance Unit (APU) (1989) *Summary Report*. London: HMSO.

Bennett, N., Desforges, C., Cockburn, A. and Wilkinson, B. (1984) *The Quality of Pupil Learning Experiences*. London: Lawrence Erlbaum Associates.

Bentley, D. (1985) *Men May Understand the Words but do they Know the Music? Some cries de Coeur in Science Education*. Paper to the Second GASAT conference, September, London.

Bentley, D. (1990) *Teaching and Learning Approaches*. Paper given as part of the Environmental Education Policy Development Symposium, Association for Science Education Annual Meeting, University of Birmingham, January.

Bentley, D. (1991) Science: the person. In Watts, D.M. (ed.) *Science in the National Curriculum*. London: Cassell.

Bentley, D. (1992a) *Fact Sheet 5, Technology Curriculum, The Times Educational Supplement Environmental Award Pack*. CREST Award Scheme, Guildford.

Bentley, D. (1992b) *Fact Sheet 6, Science Curriculum, The Times Educational Supplement Environmental Award Pack*. CREST Award Scheme, Guildford.

Bentley, D. (1992c) *Fact Sheet 7, History and Geography Curriculum, The Times Educational Supplement Environmental Award Pack*. CREST Award Scheme, Guildford.

Bentley, D. (1993) *An evaluation of GETSET*. Mimeograph, Roehampton Institute, London.

Bentley, D. and Watts, D.M. (1989) *Learning and Teaching in School Science: Practical Alternatives*. Milton Keynes: Open University Press.

Bentley, D. and Watts, D.M. (1994) *Primary Science and Technology: Practical Alternatives*. Milton Keynes: Open University Press.

Bentley, D., Ellington, K. and Stewart, D (1985) Some SSCR philosophies of Science Education. *School Science Education*, **66**, **237**, 685–667.

Birke, L. (1992) Inside Science for women: Common Sense or science? *Journal For Higher Education*, **16**, 3.

Burrows, P. (1984) The Pimlico Chemistry Trail. *School Science Review*, **66**, **235**, 221–223.

Budgett-Meakin, C.E.A. (ed.) (1992) *Make the Future Work*. London: Longmans.

Carre, C. (1981) *Language, Teaching and Learning Science*. London: Ward Lock Educational.

Calderhead, J. (1984) *Teachers' Classroom Decision-Making*. London: Holt.

Cawthorne, E.R. and Rowell, J.A. (1978) Epistemology and science education. *Studies in Science Education*, **5**, 31–59.

Chambers, J. (1989) *Pathways to Partnership: Module 5 – problem solving with industry*. INDTEL, Headway House, Christie Estate, Ivy Road, Aldershot, Hants.

Cohen, S. and Taylor, L. (1972) *Psychological Survival*. London: Penguin Books.

Chemistry for Science Teachers: Theme 5 – The environment (1992) Milton Keynes: Open University Press.

Cluster Links Project (1992) C/o Ann Adams/Dave Ashton, Castle Tertiary College, Granville Road, Sheffield, S2 2RL.

CREST Awards Scheme (1992) *CREST 1992 Gold Awards Participants Booklet and Agenda*. Guildford: CREST Awards Scheme.

CREST Awards Scheme (1993) *CREST 1993 Gold Awards Participants Booklet and Agenda*. Guildford: CREST Awards Scheme.

DeBono, E. (1978) *Teaching Thinking*. London: Pelican Books.

Desforge, C. (ed) (1989) *Early Childhood Education*. Edinburgh: Scottish Academic Press.

Department of Education and Science (DES) (1990) *National Curriculum Technology*. London: HMSO.

Department for Education (DFE) (1993) *Examination Statistics GCSE and A-level, 1992*. London: HMSO.

Dewey, J. (1919) *How we Think*. Boston: Heath.

Driver, D., Guesne, E. and Tiberghien, A. (1985) *Childrens' Ideas in Science*. Milton Keynes: Open University Press.

Edwards, P., Watts, D.M. and West, A. (1993) *Making the Difference*. Godalming: World Wide Fund for Nature.

ELAPEF 2 (1993) *II Escola Latin American sobre Pesquisa de Ensinio de Fisica*. Canela, Rio Grande do Sul, Brasil, July.

Exciting Science and Engineering Project (1991) The Chemical Industry Education Centre, University of York, York.

Experimenting with Industry Projects (1985) London: SCSST/ASE.

Eyre, D. (1993) Able children in state schools: Some reflections. *Newsletter of the National Association for Gifted Children*, Spring.

Fisher, R. (1989) *Problem solving in primary schools*. Oxford: Blackwell.

Gagne, R.M. (1970) *The Conditions of Learning*. London: Holt-Saunders.

Gibbs, G. (1988) *Learning by Doing. A Guide to Teaching and Learning Methods*. London: Further Education Unit.

Gilbert, J.K. and Watts, D.M. (1983) Conceptions, misconceptions and alternative conceptions: changing perspectives in science education. *Studies in Science Education*, **10**, 61–98.

Good Ideas for EIU (1992) SCIP, Centre for Education and Industry, University of Warwick, Coventry, CV4 7AL.

Griffiths, D. (1976) Women and science. A woman replies. In Hinton, K. (ed) *Women and Science. SISCON Project*. Hatfield: Association for Science Education.

Hari-Augustein, S. and Thomas, L. (1991) *Learning Conversations*. London: Routledge.

Harrison, W. and Nicholson, A. (1993) Company documents as educational resources. *Education in Science, July*.

Harrison, W. and Ramsden, P. (1992) Chapter 2: Where do we start from, theory or Practice? *Open Chemistry, Chemistry for Science Teachers*. London: Hodder and Staoughton.

Health Matters Project (1990) Consortium of East Hull Schools, c/o Chris Conoley, Wilberforce Sixth Form College, Salthouse Road, Hull, Yorks.

Her Majesty's Inspectors (HMI) (1978) *Primary Education in England*. London: HMSO.

Her Majesty's Inspectors (HMI) (1992) *Provision for Pupils with Emotional and Behavioural Difficulties in Special Schools*. London: HMSO.

HMSO (1981) *Special Needs in Education: The 1981 Education Act*. London: HMSO.

HMSO (1993) *Choice and Diversity, The 1993 Education Act*. London: HMSO.

Instone, I. (1988) *The Teaching of Problem Solving*. London: Longman.

Interactive Chemistry Teaching Packages (ICTP) (1977) Scottish Education Department, Glasgow University.

Intermediate Technology (1993) *Strategies and Guidelines* IT Education Office, Intermediate Technology, Myson House, Railway Terrace, Rugby CV21 3HT.

Jackson, K.F. (1983) *The Art of Solving Problems*. Reading: Bulmershe College.

Johnsey, R. (1986) *Problem Solving in School Science*. London: MacDonald Educational.

Kelly, A. (1987) *Science for Girls?* Milton Keynes: Open University Press.

Kolb, D.A. (1984) *Experiential Learning - Experience as the Source of Learning and Development*. New Jersey: Prentice Hall.

Larkin, J. (1980) *The Cognition of Learning Physics*. Applied Cognitive Psychology Paper No. 1, Department of Psychology, Carnegie Mellon University, Pittsburgh.

Lawton, D. (1983) *Curriculum Studies and Educational Planning: Studies in Teaching and Learning Series*. London: Hodder and Stoughton.

Layton, D. (1991) Science education and praxis: the relationship of school science to practical action. *Studies in Science Education*, **19**, 43–79.

Liebschner, H.P.J. (1992) *A Child's Work. Freedom and Guidance in Froebel's Educational Theory and Practice*. Cambridge: The Lutterworth Press.

Manthorpe, C. (1982) Feminists look at science. *New Scientist*, **108**, 29–31.

Mayer, R.E. (1977) *Thinking and Problem Solving: An Introduction to Human Cognition and Learning*. Illinois: Scott, Foresman Co.

Munson, P. (1988) Some thoughts on problem solving. In: Heaney, J. and Watts, D. M. (eds) *Problem Solving: Ideas and Approaches from the Secondary Science Curriculum Review*. Harlow: Longman for Schools Curriculum Development Committee.

Murphy, P. (1988) Gender differences in pupils' reactions to practical work. In B. Woolnough (ed) *Practical Science*. Milton Keynes: Open Univesity Press.

NCC (National Curriculum Council) (1990) *Curriculum Guidance 7: Environmental Education*. York: National Curriculum Council.

NCC (National Curriculum Council) (1991a) *Technology in the National Curriculum*. York: National Curriculum Council.

NCC (National Curriculum Council) (1991b) *Science in the National Curriculum*. York: National Curriculum Council.

PAST-16 (1992) *Problem Solving Past 16*. Hatfield/London: Association for Science Education/Employment Department.

PSI (Problem solving with industry) Project (1990) Centre for Science Education. Sheffield Hallam University, Sheffield.

Rea, V. and Martin, M. (1991 and 1993) Global Contexts for the National Curriculum - 1. *Stove Maker, Stove User*, 2. *Rural Blacksmith, Rural Businessman*, and 3. *Creating Art, Creating Income*. Rugby: Intermediate Technology Publications.

Robertson, C. (1991) Pupils of Marked Aptitude. *Gifted Education International*, 7(3), 149–150.

Rogoff, B. (1990) *Apprenticeship in Thinking*. Oxford: Oxford University Press.

Royal Society of Chemistry (1990) *Problem solving in Chemistry*. London: RSC.

SATIS (Science and Technology in Society) Project (1986) Association for Science Education/Heinemann, London.

SCIPSIMS Series (1991) SCIP, Centre for Education and Industry, University of Warwick, Coventry, CV4 7AL.

SEAC (School Examination and Assessment Council) (1992) *The Assessment of Performance in Design and Technology.* London: HMSO.

Science with Technology Project (1993) Association for Science Education/Design Technology Association, Hatfield, London.

Schumacher, E. (1972) *Small is Beautiful.* London: Abacus.

Schwartz, J.L. (1983) Intellectual tools for the manipulation of precepts and concepts. In *Proceedings of US-Italy Joint Seminar on Science Education for Elementary School Children.* Frascati, Italy, October 1983.

Skilbeck, M. (1976) *Ideologies and Values, Unit 3 of Course E203, Curriculum Design and Development.* Milton Keynes: Open University.

Secondary Science Curriculum Review (1985) *Better Science, Curriculum Guides 1-10.* London/Hatfield: Heinemann/Association for Science Education.

Teacher Placement Service (1991) C/o Understanding British Industry, Sun alliance House, New Inn Hall Street, Oxford.

Teaching Strategies in Biotechnology Project (1987) Sheffield University, Sheffield. PAST 16 Project. Association for Science Education/Department of Employment, London.

The Challenge of Achievement (1990) Comino Foundation. Amersham, Bucks.

Turner, W.J.R. (1984) Poetry and Science. In Heath-Stubbs, J. and Salman, P. (eds) *Poems of Science.* Harmondsworth: Penguin.

Von Glaserfeld, E. (1992) A constructivist's view of teaching and learning. In Duit, R., Goldberg, F. and Niedderer, H. (eds) *Research in Physics Learning: Theoretical Issues and Empirical Studies. Proceedings of an International Workshop.* University of Bremen, March 4-8, 1991.

Walsh, A.S. (1992) *A Study of the Concept of Design and Technology Capability.* Unpublished MA dissertation, Roehampton Institute and University of Surrey.

Warnock, J. (1993) Special Educational Needs: the real integration story. *Times Educational Supplement,* **April.**

Watts, D.M. (1991) *The Science of Problem Solving.* London: Cassell.

Watts, D.M. (1992) *Fact sheet 3: 'Getting Going' The Times Educational Supplement Environmental Award Pack.* CREST Award Scheme, Guildford.

Watts, D.M. and Bentley, D. (1994) Humanising and feminising school science. *International Journal of Science Education,* **16**(1) 83-97.

West, A. and Chandaman, R. (1993) The Real Gold Standard. *Physics Education,* **28**, 274-283.

White legge, E, Murphy, P., Scanlon, E. and Hodgson, B. (1994) Groupwork in science investigations: do boys and girls do it differently?

In Bentley, D. and Watts, D.M. (eds) *Primary Science and Technology*. Milton Keynes: Open University Press.

Woolnough, B. and Allsop, T. (1985) *Practical Work in Science*. Cambridge Science Education Series. Cambridge: Cambridge University Press.

Zachary, D. (1991) Science and the maths curriculum. In Watts, D.M. (ed.) *Science in the National Curriculum*. London: Cassell.

Zylbersztajn, A. (1983) *Conceptual Frameworks for Science Education: Investigating Curriculum Materials and Classroom Interaction in Secondary School Physics*. Unpublished PhD Thesis, University of Surrey.

Index

151